THE TYRANT OF SIENA

HEROES OF FLORENCE

By Jude Mahoney

First Kindle edition 2012

©2012 Jude Mahoney

Also by Jude Mahoney:

The Ottoman Scourge

The Field of Miracles

The Heretics' Hellfire

Stormboar

The year is 1483 and the war with Siena ended in
stalemate but now a new, more powerful threat has risen
from the east and the spectre of death and destruction
yet again hangs over Florence and her allies. Knight and
hero of Florence, Giovanni Lascorza and his chief aide,
Otto Baldwinson are forced to travel to Venice to trace
the last known whereabouts of their friend Isabella, lest

she suffer the wrath of a vengeful old enemy.

In Giovanni Lascorza and the Ottoman Scourge, mighty empires clash as the Ottoman hordes seek to overthrow and annihilate the ancient Republic of Venice whilst a priceless artefact lies at the centre of a power struggle which will determine the fate of the known world. In the midst of the fray Giovanni and Otto arrive and a desperate struggle for survival ensues.

15th Century Florence

Our story takes place in northern Italy in the late Fifteenth Century during a time of political intrigue and considerable social debauchery. It was an age of religious flux and military strife, yet it was also a period of great personal enlightenment, of humanist development and of great works of art and sculpture the likes of which had not been seen for over a thousand years. Set against the tumultuous backdrop of the Black Death that had preceded it, individual warring city states vied for power amongst their rivals. Our heroes Giovanni Lascorza and Otto Baldwinson lived lives of mixed fortune but also of great adventure and heroism. Here now, dear friends, is their tale.

PROLOGUE

A lone pair of predatory eyes watched its prey from the protective darkness of the alleyway. The predator, for that was what he was, had tracked his victim for several days now, carefully watching, spying and ensuring that his target was in fact, the right man; nothing had been left to chance. From the gutters and shadows he'd watched and waited for the right moment to strike and to leave his mark.

His target, a wealthy and well-connected merchant, was attired in his finest clothes and equipped with his most ornate dagger and jewels. Ferrante Uccello was a man on the make, a rising star and an increasingly influential merchant who took a great and selfish pride in his meteoric rise to tremendous wealth. It has been said that greed has long been the ruin of many a man and it was certainly the case here. Eventually, after calming his own suspicions that he was being followed, Uccello began day dreaming of the wine and whores he would purchase to satiate his desires. He had acquired increasingly expensive tastes as his imports business from the Orient had become more and more successful and, although he had created many new enemies, he lived in a near permanent state of revelry and merriment, oblivious to the hateful stares he received in the courts of Florence.

His avaricious thoughts turned briefly to his wife and mistress, for he would have to ensure that neither was aware of the other if he were to continue the easy life of opulence to which he was fast becoming accustomed. His wife was plain and dependable but he'd long since lost interest in her over the years, his mistress, however, lit a lustful passion in him that he was not man enough to resist. Those same thoughts were etched across his face for he could not hide the sneering grin that had spread across it.

In that moment of inner gloating, the wealthy merchant failed to see a hand as it reached from behind and slipped a thin wire around his throat. The last thing he saw was the bright, azure sky as his head was jerked brutally back and the lethal grip tightened. His arms flailed wildly as he grabbed frantically at the wire that sliced effortlessly through muscle and bone. Gasping for breath and fighting for his very life, he was dragged into a nearby alleyway. His death groans and life force faded to naught and to be doubly sure, the assassin slipped a long, serrated blade into his prey, over and over and over again, and with that, the merchant slumped, wide and vacant eyed, to the cobbles. Seconds later his vile deed done, the assassin slipped back into the shadows and vanished as though nothing had ever happened.

Republic of Florence, summer, 1483

The soft rumble of distant thunder rolled across the horizon and the pitter-patter of rain fell on the sill of the open window ledge. Inside, the small stone cell reeked of carnal lust and incense and this in turn mixed with the cool earthy air that always followed such a storm. From a low hanging branch near the window, a dove cooed gently.

The stone cell was sparse and grey, with only a small bed with a straw mattress in the one corner and a wooden crucifix on the wall opposite the entrance. On the bed lay two entwined lovers, their sweating, heaving skin open shamelessly to the world.

It was more than an hour after dawn and the other young novitiates in the seminary had long since risen from their beds and begun their daily prayers, with the exception of one.

A heavy pounding at the door woke both from their sensual slumber.

"Open this door! Open up at once!"

"Shit!" the young man sat bolt upright, his heart pounding in his chest. "Where's my bloody shirt?" he said fumbling for the white linen shirt that lay on the stone floor.

His lover, a young buxom wench from a nearby outlying village that lay less than half a day's ride from Florence barely stirred. Instead she smiled, yawned and stretched out fully, like a cat woken from its sleep.

"Open up in the name of the Abbott!" said the angry voice from outside again, followed immediately by the sound of heavy iron keys being forced into the lock.

The heavy door flew open and slammed against the stone wall.

"What in God's *name*, do we have here?" said an elderly priest, his age wizened eyes scrunched up tight.

"I can explain everything…" said the young man, with one arm in his under shirt and the other covering his crotch.

"Can you, *truly*?" said the priest.

The young man winced.

"In a word, *no*."

It was at this point that the elderly priest turned his steely gaze upon the woman who was still draped, naked across the bed.

"You *dare* bring a whore into the house of God?" scorned the priest.

"She's *no* whore, her name is Fabiana. Fabiana, this is Father Petrus, Father Petrus, meet Fabiana."

The elderly priest bristled visibly; Fabiana smiled nervously and raised her hand in acknowledgement.

"Giovanni Lascorza, you may have your father's wit, if only it were true that you had half of his ability," the priest retorted.

It wasn't often that the young, mercurial Lascorza took offence but the obvious slight and comparison with his father left him clenching his jaw.

The priest continued, ignoring Giovanni's discomfort. "I watch and pray so that you will not fall into temptation."

"My spirit was indeed weak, but my flesh was oh *so* willing..." said Giovanni quietly, glancing at Fabiana.

"I suppose you think that's amusing, young man?" said a new voice, deeper and more authoritative than the elderly priest's.

Once again, Giovanni winced and finished dressing himself in a hurry.

"Not at all Abbott, far be it for me to be amusing in such a serious place as this," Giovanni replied.

The Abbott was a man not given to outbursts of humour, as was fitting of a man of his position. He had risen to the rank of Abbott through sheer doggedness and the key ability to outlive all of his rivals. A careful man by his very nature, he had reluctantly agreed to accept the young Giovanni Lascorza into his order as a favour to his famous and rather illustrious father, Alessandro Lascorza. Almost immediately Giovanni had proven himself to be a provocative and difficult novitiate due to his never ending questioning and inquisitive mind. Now at the age of twenty-four, the young Giovanni had become more obstinate towards him and the order than ever.

"Young Master Lascorza, there are two paths currently open to you," said the Abbott with a heavy sigh. "The first path, the right hand path one might say, is the path of *righteousness*, the path to *Godliness*; it represents your salvation and your *calling*." The Abbott paused. "The other, the *left* hand path, is the path to damnation, the

8

expulsion from this order and into the arms of this *whore*..." he spat, pointing at Fabiana.

Giovanni, still sat on the bed and only half dressed, ran his hand through his hair and sniffed.

"In that case, I choose damnation and the whore."

Palazzo Lascorza, Florence, summer 1483

Otto Baldwinson was a grizzled old veteran by any standards and had long been referred to by friends and enemies alike as *the Storm Boar,* on account of his bravery and ferocity in battle. A condottiero, he was a mercenary warrior who had found employ in the House of Lascorza for the last two decades or so, having met the head of the house, Alessandro Lascorza, when he was on a diplomatic mission from Florence to the Holy Roman Emperor, Frederick the Third. Hailing from the deep forests of Württemberg, Otto Baldwinson was a veteran of a dozen battles and almost as many personal duels. Thick set and broad, he had a fondness for fine wine and his clay pipe, through which he smoked angelikarot, a curious blend of herb grown in the far off northern lands. Rarely seen without leather armour and his famed two-handed blade that he carried propped against his shoulder, he had subsequently served the House of Lascorza faithfully as the chief aide of its master, Alessandro Lascorza.

In his youth, Alessandro Lascorza had been a vigorous man, firm of mind and sound of judgement. As the Gonfaloniere or standard bearer of Florence, he'd been regarded as a safe choice to lead the Signoria in times of peril and, as a knight and envoy of the city in his later career, he'd travelled the length and breadth of Italy, to the distant lands of Germania, France and Spain and even for a short while at least, the remote and barbarous shores of England. He was, in short, a great man of stature. Possessed of an explorer's mind Alessandro had tried to instil a sense of duty into the young Giovanni, but as a boy, he'd been more interested in daydreaming of the future than on concentrating on his studies.

The household Alessandro inherited, it was fair to say, had suffered from mixed fortunes despite its noble status. The lady of the house, Giovanni's mother, had died in childbirth, giving birth to Giovanni's youngest sister, Cordelia and other, darker secrets haunted the already troubled home. It was all Alessandro could do to hold the family together through sheer force of will, although he could in no way entertain the notion of remarrying, so in love was he with his late wife. Otto often saw his master and friend weep into the small hours but said nothing. He'd watched as the young and vulnerable Giovanni had grown up without a mother, and tried to take him under his protective influence as often as he could, teaching him the ways of the sword and the knight's path. Despite his own innate, deep faith in the Almighty, Otto had counselled Alessandro Lascorza against forcing Giovanni into joining the ranks of the priesthood, sensing that his destiny lay along a different path.

For twenty years, Otto had walked the streets of Florence and called it home. The city, even with its revitalised patronisation of the arts still bore the hallmarks of a city of its time. Regardless of the fine art that adorned the walls of its streets, the horse shit that lay in the road, the mutton and other cooking fats that spilled out into the gutters, the stench of rotting vegetables and body odour of its unwashed and impure citizenry reminded all who entered that it was no better or worse than any other city of the age. Through the stench of those streets, Otto now found himself, having received word of Giovanni's expulsion from the seminary. He trod his way carefully over the effluence covered cobble stones and through darkened side streets, until at last he happened upon the outskirts of the seminary. With a deep breath, he forced his shoulders back and headed towards the main entrance.

The seminary was a magnificent, imposing building, fortress like in its appearance, it was low and square shaped, surrounding a central courtyard. Fully enveloped by trees, it was a picturesque sight to behold. Upon entering the seminary, a young novitiate going about his business caught Otto's eye.

"Excuse me, would you tell me where I might find Master Giovanni Lascorza of the House Lascorza?" said Otto with a feigned air of politeness.

The novitiate, surprised at seeing the roguish bulk of Otto, stared in wide amazement.

"He left, a day or so ago. I was under the impression he'd taken up residence somewhere in the San Lorenzo district," stuttered the young man.

Otto sighed deeply, annoyed at having missed Giovanni and dismayed that he'd been right all along having instinctively known that the young Lascorza would make a terrible priest.

"Thank you, I'll have word sent to him at once," said Otto glumly before making his way from the seminary and back out into the street.

The truth was such that he bore the young master yet more ill news. Giovanni's father had lain upon his deathbed for the previous two days. Although Otto's old master was a hardy man capable of great acts of bravery and stamina, he was older and frailer now and despite the best efforts of the local physicians who'd practised all sorts of medicine upon his old frame, all had failed. His health was clearly failing and some of the household servants had talked in hushed voices of witchcraft or poisoning although none could verify the truth of such claims and none would be so bold as to speak openly of such things.

With a heavy heart and an uncertain mind, Otto grabbed a nearby boy by the shoulder.

"I would have you carry word to a friend of mine in the San Lorenzo district. Can you do this for me?" he said.

The terrified urchin was grubby faced and painfully thin, typical of the pauper families that lived in utter squalor and deprivation along the banks of the Arno. Their existence was short and typically brutal but for all the child's earthy demeanour, Otto knew that the small gold coin he placed in the child's hand would have been more money than he'd ever seen and would in turn, ensure his loyalty.

"Go to the San Lorenzo district; there you will enquire after a Master Giovanni Lascorza and his location.

13

When you find him, tell him that he must return home at once, it is a matter of urgency."

His mucous and grime stained face looked glum as he replied. "What should I tell him if he asks what the urgent matter is?"

It was a valid question and the old condotierro could not find it within himself to scold the boy for asking personal questions.

Otto sighed.

"You may tell him…" he paused, "that his father isn't long for this world."

The boy stared up at Otto open-mouthed. Saying nothing, he nodded and darted off, heading north through the labyrinthine streets of the old city.

Otto's gaze followed the boy as he disappeared into the crowds. His work done, he returned home, following the darker, less densely packed side alleys and streets and arrived a quarter of an hour later outside the gates of the Palazzo Lascorza.

The mood in the household was sombre, yet the servants and aides that ran the extensive palazzo went about their business as expected. As the head of the household's chief aide and close personal friend, Otto, was afforded much in the way of respect from the rest of the staff and close access to Alessandro Lascorza. Entering through the main gate he made his way up to his master's private bedchambers through the main banqueting hall and up through the master staircase. Along the way, numerous painting of the illustrious noble family's ancestors adorned the walls, and the family's personal heraldry was on display for all to see.

Otto slowed his pace as he reached the private bed chambers of his master. Outside the double doors, he found one of the city's finest physicians in deep discussion with one of the family servants that Otto had employed to help run the kitchen staff. Their conversation stopped as Otto approached and an air of inevitable gloom enveloped them.

The physician, a wealthy Jew from the south of Italy, greeted Otto as he approached. Dressed in a floor length gown and a scarlet toque hat, the physician was a middle-aged man with a weather beaten face and in his role he'd seen many an ailment and served the citizenry and noble classes of Florence for many years.

"Otto, the news isn't good. His condition isn't improving and if there exists *any* medicine in this world that can save him, I'm afraid it is beyond me."

Otto nodded glumly and placed his hand on the physician's shoulder.

"You've tried your best, I'm sure of that. Now it is in God's hands alone," replied Otto.

"I have bled him and have used my finest leeches, combined with some secret concoctions known only to the ancients, all to no avail." The physician lowered his head as though he felt the failure to heal the elderly Lascorza personally.

The corridor outside the bedchamber was dimly lit, and even though it was daylight outside and the stifling heat of late summer made everyone sweat, all of the windows were closed and the curtains were drawn tightly together.

Otto knocked on his master's bedchamber door and walked into darkness. Inside the room, a personal attendant of the master of the household stood fanning the elder Lascorza as he lay in his bed.

Adorned in his finest silk bed clothes, Alessandro Lascorza lay semi upright with a dozen fine silk pillows packed behind his back. Rose petal water lay in small wooden bowls around the room, adding some scented respite to the stultifying and oppressive darkness and heat.

Otto approached the bed slowly, and stopped some feet from it, whereby he coughed politely and waited his turn to speak.

The old man in the bed opened his eyes briefly and turned slowly to face his old aide.

Otto smiled warmly even though he doubted the elder Lascorza could see him.

"I've some grave news old friend," Otto paused. "Your son has left the seminary and has taken up lodgings in the north of the city."

It was hard to see the disappointment on a dying man's face and know how best to react, erring on the side of caution, Otto remained tight-lipped and it was his master who sighed and replied.

"Should've bloody well listened to you, Otto. You always did know best," groaned the old Lascorza, his voice gravelly and thick with tension.

Otto took a sharp intake of breath and placed his hands behind his back.

"I sent a messenger for him to the San Lorenzo district, I'm sure he'll be with us very soon," he replied trying to sound hopeful.

Alessandro laughed and immediately began to cough.

Otto stooped forward to assist the old man and was immediately shooed away from him.

"I may be old and dying, but I don't need a nursemaid quite yet," he said jovially although he'd coughed flecks of blood onto the white handkerchief he kept in his right hand.

With a light hearted laugh that betrayed his true feelings, Otto nodded.

"I recall that only too well old friend; you certainly didn't need a nursemaid when you saved my arse from the hands of the French, or during those soured negotiations with the Holy Roman Empire," said Otto barely able to suppress his laughter.

"I recall many other times besides those too, Otto Baldwinson," said the frail elder Lascorza.

Otto smiled and nodded and at once felt both helpless and angry. Although Alessandro Lascorza was advanced in years, his premature plight was almost certainly unnatural and Otto's finely honed instincts suspected foul play, even though he could not prove it.

"When my son arrives, have him sent to me at once, there are many things left unsaid that I would say to him. There were many things said in anger that a father

17

ought not to have said to his son," said Alessandro with a laboured breath.

Otto nodded his agreement. He had known of their ill words spoken before Giovanni's entry to the seminary. A blazing row of epic proportions had seen father and son who'd never been especially close fall ever further apart. He recalled their final parting words of anger and resentment and wondered privately if anything might be salvaged from it. It seemed for the longest while that nothing would be done, and now, in those current circumstances, Otto hoped and prayed that Giovanni would swallow his pride and return home.

The heavy weight of his two-handed blade caused Otto's shoulders to ache. With a mild sense of relief, he hoisted the heavy blade over his head and propped it gently against the wall near his master's bed. He picked up a white handkerchief that lay on the table next to Alessandro's bed and dipped it gently into some rose petal water before dabbing it on his master's brow.

"Alessandro, you ought not to be so harsh on yourself. You raised a hero, a stubborn, obstinate young man, just like you used to be," smiled Otto.

San Lorenzo district, Florence, summer 1483
It was during the long, sweltering hot summer of 1483 that Giovanni Lascorza had first been informed of his father's impending demise. A small boy had approached him as he sat outside a tavern, enjoying the last of his coin that had been spent on a lavish meal. The urchin who

could have been no older than six or seven had, when asked, told him that his father lay dying and insisted that Giovanni was to hurry at once to see him. Giovanni glanced around, wondering if it were some sick and awful prank being played upon him, the realisation that it was not, left him feeling winded and nauseous.

Deep in thought, Giovanni recalled the last time he and his father had spoken and was only vaguely aware of the musicians playing on their lutes and lyres, serenading young couples in exchange for coin and a minute's fame. The bright sunlight played on the pale cream buildings, dazzling onlookers and producing deep shadows in doorways and window recesses. Giovanni's recollections were returned to the present by the familiar, fragrant scent of rose bushes in the Via Ricasoli.

As he approached his ancestral home, Giovanni took a deep breath, closed his eyes and walked into the courtyard of his childhood. In the centre of the courtyard stood a small fountain; the noise of flowing water splashing into a marble basin echoed around the enclosed area and, with the assistance of a summer breeze, it was possible to smell the faint perfume of nearby rose bushes and lavender. The garden, edged with gravel and stone walkways, was diligently tended by several gardeners whose job it was to weed, water, and create perfection in an otherwise arid environment.

In the corner, weeping quietly and being comforted by a member of the household, was Giovanni's youngest sister, Cordelia Lascorza; sensitive, tender in nature and dressed in a deep, royal blue, she was several years younger than Giovanni. Being blessed with a keen intellect, she was also in possession of wisdom far beyond her years.

Passing through the heavily reinforced gates into the courtyard, Giovanni spied his sister and immediately proceeded towards her. Seeing her brother, Cordelia Lascorza smiled, but for all the sentiment, Giovanni knew her well enough to sense her underlying grief and pain. He greeted his sister and held her in a consoling and tender manner.

As he kissed her on her forehead, a voice rang out over the courtyard, echoing as it did so. "Giovanni!"

Giovanni turned to see his father's old friend and aide, Otto Baldwinson, a bull of a man, thick set yet immaculately turned out and dressed in his familiar leather armour emblazoned with the Lascorza family crest.

"Otto! It's been too long, how are you keeping?" Giovanni replied.

"I'm fine. Your father however has seen better days; this was... sudden, to say the least."

Otto searched Giovanni's face for any trace of emotion. The two men shook hands as old friends before turning and walking side-by-side up a steep flight of stone steps and into the elder Lascorza's chambers.

Before entering the bed chamber, Otto turned to Giovanni and spoke, "Giovanni, he is close to passing. It will be painful for you to see him like this, but better you see him as he is now than not at all." Otto paused briefly, carefully choosing his next words. "There is another matter. Word of your father's failing health has reached the Signoria. It appears there is something of great importance that they wish to discuss with you."

"*Me*?" Giovanni replied. "What would they want with me?"

"Giovanni, you are your father's son. You have far more ability than you give yourself credit for. If the Signoria have a matter of great urgency that they wish to discuss with you, it is because they have great faith in you and recognise your abilities, your worth, more so perhaps, than you do yourself."

"And should I refuse? What then? If whatever they should ask of me is beyond my ability, or so dangerous that I should refuse it, what then? Why should I do anything for this city? How and what do I gain from it, precisely?"

Sensing the finality in this question and realising the futility in continuing, Otto nodded gravely and stood aside to let Giovanni pass. Giovanni held Otto's gaze for the briefest of moments before entering the all-consuming darkness of his father's bed chamber.

"Father...?"

"Giovanni?" a strained voice replied. "My son, thank God you came. I feared that you would not."

"Father, I—"

"You have no need to apologise my son; the fault is mine. I ought to have listened to you and your pleas; alas, it is my failing as a father that I could not and would not listen to my only God-given boy."

Giovanni sat in silence, stunned by his father's words, and realised how difficult life must have been for him, looking after both himself and his two sisters after their mother had passed away. It was hard to rationalise the feelings he'd had at that time, guilt, love, admiration, despair vied with each other in his private thoughts.

Weeping gently, Giovanni realised that he had had so much to say, so much anger and bitterness to vent, and now, given the chance, he could not find the words. They had stuck in his throat and he could find no voice at all. Holding his father's fragile frame, he leant in closer as the old man struggled for breath.

"I have left you what I could... you will be informed of the details after I have gone to meet my maker. Otto, my aide and dear friend, has pledged to serve you now, and I know that he will assist you as ably and loyally as he has me. Giovanni, you are my heir, the *last* of the male Lascorza's, and I have every faith in you. You are not the sum of your past, the *future* is not yet set in stone, and you must concentrate on the present. Serve Florence, as I have done; it falls to you now to uphold the family honour and name. I—"

With his breathing becoming increasingly more erratic and strained, Alessandro's words became more and more halting. At last, unable to speak anymore, he held Giovanni's hand. Their eyes locked; the sentiment passing between them expressing far more in that final moment than words ever could.

Finally, trembling from supressed emotion, Giovanni placed his right hand over his father's waxen face and closed his father's eyes. Remorsefully he stood up from his father's still body, took a deep breath and ran his hands through his long, thick, jet black hair. A swelling upsurge of primal emotion flooded through him. So many thoughts, memories and feelings came to the fore all at once, so many in fact, that he little knew what to do or how to act. His legs buckling beneath him, he sat down on the floor, placed his head on his knees and wept, allowing the walls around his emotions to disintegrate for the first time since his mother's death. He sat thus, in the darkened room, until the well of his grief had run dry and there were no more tears left to cry.

Eventually, having regained some semblance of composure, Giovanni opened the curtains that had held the room in sombre darkness. A brilliant shaft of early afternoon sun flooded the room illuminating the figure in the bed. Turning to leave, he looked back one last time at his father. He walked over to the bed and placed a tender kiss on his gaunt cheek before returning to the courtyard below to find the ever dependable Otto waiting.

Moving from the shade of the house into brilliant sunshine, Giovanni stopped a few feet away from Otto, who wore his two-handed sword around his back and held a second sword, with the tip of its blade pointed towards the ground. With a practised ease, the older man rested a reassuring gauntleted hand on Giovanni's shoulder, "I have pledged to serve you as I once did your father. You may be assured that I will serve you until my last breath and the very last beat of my heart, but for now

I will take care of the necessary arrangements for your father's funeral; there will be much to do. However, there is still the matter of the business with the Signoria that you must also attend to."

"Oh?" Giovanni replied.

"Yes, at the very least they will wish to pass on their condolences, your father was greatly respected and well-liked."

Otto paused. "There is a matter of grave importance that they wish to discuss with you. They are men of great power and influence and ought not to be kept waiting for too long. Although your service is not expected, redemption and salvation are powerful, motivating forces, Giovanni. You would do well to remember that. Perhaps you might, one day, lay the ghosts of your past to rest in the service of this city."

"Perhaps," Giovanni muttered as he made to pass Otto.

Otto stopped his young master, taking him by the shoulder, before throwing a sword that he held in a reverse grip to the ground.

"Before we go anywhere, I want to see how much you recall from your youth," said Otto.

There was a flash of tension in the courtyard and neither man would look away first.

"Pick it up," said Otto as he flung the longsword onto the ground.

"You would speak to *me* in such a manner?" said Giovanni indignantly as he ambled towards the blade.

The palazzo staff sensed what was coming and quickly scurried away back into the palazzo.

"Your education, young man, begins *here*. I may be your aide, which puts me in the service of both you and this esteemed house, but you have much to learn about leadership. Your father knew how to lead, now *you* must learn too," he said whilst circling Giovanni.

Picking up the blade, Giovanni drew the sword from its scabbard and held the blade before him. With his gaze fixed firmly upon the ground, he tentatively placed the scabbard down as Otto rushed forward and kneed him in the face.

Crashing to the ground, Giovanni clutched his face as a slow trickle of blood oozed from his nose.

"You forget yourself," he said. "Do that again and I shall have you whipped."

"As I said, I may *be* in the service of this house but I am not your slave, I am not your lackey and I am most certainly not your whipping boy. Now, get to your feet," growled Otto as he continued circling Giovanni.

"You have in your hand, a longsword. You played with them in your youth, but as you no longer belong in the priesthood, you had better damn well acquaint yourself with one; it might one day save your life. Do you understand?"

Giovanni nodded as he rose unsteadily to his feet. Otto swung his great two-handed blade in a diagonal arc from his top right to bottom left as his young opponent leapt back in one fluid motion.

25

"Good, you can move quickly. Footwork is key," continued Otto.

"As is balance!" continued Otto as he thrust his blade forward forcing Giovanni to retreat again. This time, however, Giovanni tripped as he fell over a rosebush in the palazzo courtyard.

Giovanni grimaced as he rubbed his sore back. "You could take it easy on me," he complained.

"You think your enemies will?" said Otto.

"I have no enemies," Giovanni shot back as he held his blade in front of him.

"Not yet you don't, give it time and life will find you," said Otto as he launched another great arching attack. Again Giovanni dodged the blow and leapt backwards to give himself space.

"Don't move away from my blade, you weren't raised a coward!" growled Otto.

Beads of sweat ran down Giovanni's brow like raindrops flowing down a window during a storm. "I want to stop for water," said Giovanni breathing heavily.

"No water!" cried Otto as he kicked out with his right foot. The blow connected with Giovanni's left leg and sent him tumbling to the ground, and this time, Otto was in no mood to show any mercy. The old condotierro planted both feet either side of Giovanni's chest and held the tip of his blade to his young master's chest.

"There is *no* mercy to be had on the field of battle. There are *no* friends, only enemies and blood. Learn enough today, and hopefully it won't be your blood being shed," said Otto as he moved his sword to one side and offered Giovanni a hand up.

"You will teach me the ways of the longsword?" said Giovanni.

"I will teach you the ways of the *German* longsword and I will *teach* you the knightly path. I will instruct you in the way that I was by my master," replied Otto.

The courtyard in which they stood was the courtyard that Giovanni remembered from his youth, it was through the windows of the top floor library where he would watch Otto and his father practise their sword play. The memory flashed into his thoughts and he smiled as he noticed some of the household staff peeking through the windows of the lower floors.

"I would gladly accept, what must I do?" said Giovanni, aware that he was being watched.

For the first time, Otto smiled. "Take a knee young one, and repeat after me..."

Giovanni tentatively knelt before Otto, and bowed his head as though in deep and reverent prayer.

Otto held out his hand and placed it gently on Giovanni's head.

"Young knight, learn to love God and honour noble women, so grows your honour, practise chivalry and learn art which adorns you and will glorify you in battle."

Giovanni made to move his head, but Otto held it in place. "Now you," said Otto.

"I shall learn to love God, honour the nobility of *all* women, I will make chivalry my art and in battle, I shall bring the mercy of angels to my foe," said Giovanni as though the words came to him as naturally as could be.

"Good," said Otto. "Then rise to your feet, and hold your sword like this," he continued as he held his two-handed blade above his head so that it protruded forward, pointing at Giovanni.

"You will learn the four guards, all five master strikes and every technique handed down from Johannes Liechenaur to my master, the great Hans Talhoffer. We shall begin with Ochs. Are you ready?"

Giovanni nodded, rose to his feet and held his blade above his head, pointing forward. In a crouched position, he held the guard and copied Otto's every move.

"What about your sword, when will I have my own blade such as that?" said Giovanni an hour later.

"It takes a great man to wield a great sword. You have not yet made a name for yourself. It would be unfitting for you to have a sword of Gertrude's stature at your age."

"*Gertrude*? Your sword is called *Gertrude*?" said Giovanni with a suppressed grin.

Otto paused and lowered his guard, his visage was grim.

"Yes, what of it?" he said.

"Nothing, I'm sure it's a perfectly suitable name for a sword," said Giovanni, now openly grinning.

"It was my mother's name, if you find that *amusing*, perhaps you would like to challenge me as you feel your training is complete?" said Otto.

"You should remember your place old man," said Giovanni as he crouched and held his blade in the Ochs guard.

Otto shook his head. "So be it, young master. When I am finished here, you will learn that with leadership comes humility and pride almost *always* comes before a fall."

For an older man, Otto moved with a speed that surprised Giovanni. So much so that Giovanni was still thinking as such as Otto's blade lashed out towards his face and came within a whisker of slicing him open. The next blow hammered down on Giovanni's blade and then a second time from a different angle. Giovanni was again forced backwards against the edge of the courtyard and upon the third blow against his blade; the sword was skilfully wrenched from his hand and span off several feet away from him. Otto barely breathed, in his concentration and fear, Giovanni's chest rose and fell heavily.

"I serve you willingly as I did your father but do not abuse those who serve you. There is warmth in kindness and sanctuary in friendship. I will offer you both," said Otto as he lowered Gertrude onto his shoulder.

Giovanni nodded. Having led such a privileged existence, was unused to servants within his household talking to him in such a gruff manner and although he had known Otto for his whole life, he had often been as distant a figure as his own father, often away accompanying him on his great adventures travelling across the known world, he realised then just why Otto was held in such high esteem both within the House of Lascorza and by his late father.

As his shoulders sank, Giovanni swallowed his pride. "I've been a fool old friend, I have need of friends, this *house* has need of friends, I should not have spoken to you in such a way."

Otto nodded and hoisted Gertrude onto his shoulder.

"A lesson well learned my lord," he smiled. "The arrangements for your father's funeral have been made, with your leave, I would see to the final details," said Otto.

The previous hour had been a distraction for Giovanni, a useful distraction, but still a ploy that Otto had used to focus Giovanni's mind on something other than his own grief.

"Life will never be the same again, will it Otto?" said Giovanni as his new aide made to leave.

"I loved him too, young master. I will do him proud as I'm sure, will *you*," smiled Otto as he bowed and walked towards the gate that led into the great hall of the palazzo.

Spying his sister, Cordelia, Giovanni picked up the scabbard of the longsword, slid the long, lethal blade back inside it and attached it to his waist.

"What will we do, brother?" said Cordelia walking towards Giovanni, her eyes red with grief.

"We will survive, we will become strong and we will flourish," said Giovanni.

Cordelia looked less than convinced. "And when the other noble houses realise our plight, what then? Will they act with kindness or circle our house with greedy, envious eyes?" she continued.

Giovanni embraced his younger sister and spoke softly. "Forget the other houses, sister. Soon you will be married and we shall forge alliances with the other houses."

Cordelia drew away from her older brother. "There is no man good enough for me. I would live out my days here, in our family home," she said sullenly.

"You will *do* what you must for the good of the family, for the good of our house!" snapped Giovanni. "Very soon I will be called to business on behalf of the Signoria. I will not be here to protect you and the household guard can only do *so* much!"

Her eyes welled up. "You are leaving? When, why?" said Cordelia.

"I don't know yet, Otto and I will hear their desires very soon," replied Giovanni.

"First father and now you, am I to be left here alone, to fend for myself?" said Cordelia.

Leading his sister by the hand, Giovanni sat down on the stone bench that lay near the ornate water fountain in the centre of the courtyard. He looked up at the carved faces of cherubim and around the edges of the arched courtyard he saw the four stone carved coats of arms that bore the family crest of the ancient House of Lascorza. Fine intricately patterned brick and marble patterns played out scenes from and paid homage to that of ancient Rome. That it was a wealthy home was apparent, designed and built to impress, it had fulfilled the role of both political statement and family home for more than a century.

"This is our home, our gates are strong, our walls are thick. Whilst your heart beats there is hope, whilst you live the soldiers of this household will fight to the finish to defend both you and it," said Giovanni.

Cordelia's face was a mask of uncertainty and Giovanni knew that his stubborn younger sister was unconvinced of his impassioned pleas.

"Besides, by marrying into another house, you will make this house stronger, that *is* what you want, isn't it?" Giovanni continued.

Cordelia sighed. "I would do whatever it took to do so, you know that. I only mourn the passing of my childhood and see only heartache in my future," she replied.

Knowing there was little he could do or say that would lighten her mood, Giovanni worried for Cordelia's wellbeing. His family had long since hidden a dark tragedy from the outside world, and public knowledge of it would have weakened their position in wider society and cast suspicion upon the House of Lascorza.

"Sister, my love, I *must* leave this place. If there is business to be had with the Signoria it will no doubt be time consuming, you have to be strong." Giovanni reached out and stroked Cordelia's hair.

Cordelia sulked and withdrew from his touch.

"Otto and I will see to things before we leave, but you must be strong, for me," said Giovanni finally as he realised the futility of his words. Turning his back on Cordelia, Giovanni made his way into the palazzo, gathered his belongings and within the half hour both he and Otto were making their way through the streets of Florence, and made for the Palazzo Vecchio, in the heart of the ancient city.

Republic of Florence, summer, 1483

As Giovanni and Otto walked through the crowded streets of the merchants' quarter, a commotion emanating from a large crowd drew their attention. The group, mainly merchants and tradesmen had gathered in one of the side alleyways and their fear was palpable as tension and near hysteria hung in the air like a cloying, heavy miasma.

"What in God's name?" Giovanni stopped and turned to his aide, "Otto, what is this?"

"No doubt something that warrants further investigation," he replied.

Easing their way through the gathered throng, they saw the reason for the murmurs and sense of fear rippling through the crowd. In the corner of the dark alleyway lay the bloodied, broken form of a man propped upright against a wall, his eyes bulging from his head, and a thin red weal oozing blood across his throat. Worse still, it was apparent that he had suffered some kind of horrific injury to his lower face.

What manner of murder is this? thought Giovanni to himself. "Otto, was this man robbed?" he commented quietly.

With a perplexed look, Otto scratched his head and muttered under his breath, "I'm not sure what this is but we should hurry, we cannot be delayed here."

Taking Otto's shoulder and stopping him in his tracks, Giovanni turned and said, "Wait, I need to know more about what happened here, who this man was, why he died in this way." The look of determination on the younger man's face spoke volumes, and Otto knew better than to attempt to stop him.

Giovanni glanced around and addressed the crowd, "Who here knew this man? Can anyone tell me his name? Did anyone hear or see anything?" Both men could clearly sense the uneasiness in the crowd, people's reluctance to come forward and speak was obvious, even if they knew little about the murder itself.

Shrugging his broad shoulders, Otto looked around and said, "Giovanni, we'll get nothing here. We should leave." Reluctantly, Giovanni agreed and both men turned, forcing their way through the mass that had continued to gather. As they did so, a voice rang out over the din of the crowd, "There is evil afoot in this city! There is evil, and the authorities are powerless to prevent it! They are unable to protect us, unable to prevent these murders! This is the third murder this month, all of the men died in this same manner."

Giovanni caught the eye of the elderly man who'd been brave enough to voice what many others present were thinking. Age had been less than kind to him, yet the man's courage was evident to see.

"My lord, I may be an old man, but even *I* know something is very wrong here. There are rumours of invasion and of treachery. The people are frightened. *I* am frightened. For my family and friends, although less so for myself. The man who was murdered here was a merchant. The others, I hear, were *also* merchants. Tell me, why do you ask about what has happened here? Are you a representative of the Signoria?" The man's searching eyes pained Giovanni, for he knew he had no real answers; at least, he realised, not yet.

Unable to hold the other man's gaze for long, Giovanni smiled and said, "I don't know, but I'm certain that the Signoria will get to the bottom of this, one way or another. You can rest assured of that."

A cynical smile passed over the lips of the elderly speaker as he half-heartedly mumbled his agreement.

Passing the chapel of San Lorenzo, Giovanni and Otto continued walking through the streets of Florence heading south into the heart of the city itself. The cream coloured buildings contrasted starkly with the terracotta roofs and the architectural magnificence of Brunelleschi loomed overhead.

The crowds had eased by the time they had arrived at the Piazza della Signoria. The wide, L-shaped forum was dominated by the crenelated tower of the enormous Palazzo Vecchio. The piazza was bathed in the brilliant afternoon sunshine which warmed their bodies, while casting shadows around the periphery of the forum itself. Giovanni and Otto walked shoulder-to-shoulder and headed for the entrance to the Palazzo Vecchio.

The large, heavily reinforced gates of the palazzo were guarded by the condottieri, the mercenary soldiers of Florence. Their surcoats, marked with the livery of the city, covered their ornate plate armour, and halberds were held high across their chests. As Giovanni and Otto approached to within mere yards of the gates, the first guard issued his challenge, "Halt, state your names and business here."

"I am Giovanni Lascorza, son of the late and former Gonfaloniere, Alessandro Lascorza, and this," he said turning to Otto, "is my aide and friend, Otto Baldwinson. We are here at the behest of the Signoria. They wish to pay their condolences to my family and, as I understand it, they have an urgent matter they wish to discuss with me."

With a curt nod, the guard replied in a heavy Swiss accent, "They have been expecting you. Step this way." Ushering the two men into a large, marble hall, the guard motioned towards their weapons. "Gentlemen, your swords; you may not take them into the presence of the Signoria."

Otto immediately consented and smiled reassuringly at Giovanni.

Walking down a long hallway they entered a vast meeting chamber. Open-mouthed, Giovanni stared around him. Paintings by some of the finest artists in the land hung from the walls lending the place an air of power and grandeur. Even with his privileged background, the young Giovanni had rarely witnessed such splendour before. Otto, observing the behaviour of the younger man, simply smiled and coughed politely, indicating that when meeting people of such influence and stature, it was preferable to not have a simpleton's open-mouthed gape. Returning the smile, Giovanni braced his shoulders, regained his equanimity and kept his mouth firmly shut.

In front of them, seated at a heavily carved wooden table sat the Council of the Nine. This was the ruling council of the city, an august oligarchy elected from the various guilds within Florence itself; well regarded by their peers, these men wielded great power within the city.

The current Gonfaloniere of Justice, a middle-aged, yet spritely man by the name of Piero Bartolo De Larosa stepped forward, his arms raised in greeting and a broad smile on his face. "Gentlemen, welcome to the Palazzo Vecchio and the Council of the Nine. The Signoria are most pleased and grateful to see you and thank you for your prompt attendance; there are many grave matters to discuss."

Bowing, both Giovanni and Otto returned their thanks at having been invited before settling down to the business at hand.

With his expression changing to one of sorrow, Gonfaloniere De Larosa said, "We are saddened to hear of the unexpected loss of your father, Giovanni. He was a good man, the best of us, in fact and he served this city well. We join you in your time of grief. If there is anything that you require of us, you have only to ask and it shall be granted." His voice echoed across the chamber.

"Thank you. Your sentiments gladden my heart," replied Giovanni, "but, there is serious business to discuss. It has been brought to our attention that there is unrest in the air. Otto and I walked past the scene of a murder on our way here. There appears to be talk of invasion and evil-doing. What does the council know of this?"

A small and slightly built, shrewd-looking man stepped forward. "My name is Salvatore Lombardi. I am the Priori of the Arte Del Cambio and what I am about to tell you must not leave this chamber. Is that understood?"

Giovanni shot a look at Otto, who merely puffed out his cheeks, shrugged his shoulders and remained impassively silent. "You have our word. Pray continue, Signor Lombardi," replied Giovanni.

Salvatore Lombardi waited for a moment, summoning up as much gravitas as his small frame could lend before continuing. "Two months ago, our spies in Pisa and Siena began reporting increased troop numbers, as well as increases in shipments of armour, weapons and other military supplies. Unusually large amounts of grain have been ferried to those cities and our suspicions have been aroused. Recently, various Florentine merchants have reported hostility towards them when conducting trade in these locations.

Even though these cities are our historical enemies, there has remained in place for a good while now an unwritten agreement that trade would continue. However, in the last month, three of our merchants have been murdered in the very heart of Florence. What we do not know is *why*... We do not believe that these are robberies; it has a darker, more sinister feel to it than that. Our early investigations have revealed that none of the merchants in question had any known enemies, but they had all recently returned from trading expeditions to Siena. This is our only clue to date. It is our hope that we could persuade you to investigate this situation and to get to the heart of this evil that threatens Florence. We are all too well known to set foot out of Florence. Our whereabouts would be immediately reported to whosoever is behind these villainous acts and ultimately, this would give the game away. We need someone with *honour*, someone *educated* and able, and someone who is a loyal servant of Florence who will uncover the real devilry here. It remains the deepest, sincerest hope of this council that you, Giovanni and you, Otto, will be those men. What do you say?"

Looking at Otto's grim face, the younger man realised that there was little choice. Giovanni smiled and replied, "Salvatore, Otto and I would be honoured to accept this responsibility. However, I would respectfully request that I be given time to lay my father to rest first, as is his due, before carrying out this undertaking."

Relieved, Lombardi merely nodded in response.

Gonfaloniere De Larosa broke the silence. "Good, then it is settled. My Lord Lascorza, you and your aide shall begin your investigations at your earliest possible convenience. You will, of course, be recompensed for any expenses that may be incurred in the course of your work."

As the two men left the Palazzo Vecchio they were initially unaware that they were being spied upon. Walking through the streets of the Via Calimala, a distinctive, menacing eyes watched both men from a distance. Otto, turning to look behind him wore a quizzical look on his face.

"What's the matter?" asked Giovanni.

"Hmm, I just had the strangest feeling we were being watched. I must be imagining things."

Evaluating their every move, the watcher trailed Giovanni and Otto as far as the Palazzo Lascorza and then watched the two men enter the building before fading away into the crowds.

Tuscan hills, summer, 1483

A day later, and some two miles to the east of Florence, outside the city walls and nestled among the nearby Tuscan hills lay the now near-derelict villa that had once been home to the Lascorza family. The former family seat had existed here in one form or another since the height of the Roman Empire but had not been formally lived in for many years, the family preferring the palazzo within the city walls. The villa, for all its dilapidation, remained a place of sanctity for the family. It was in these grounds that the family tombs were situated. Great stone mausoleums of illustrious Lascorza ancestors were scattered just out of view of the old house, a constant reminder of vast power, wealth and timeless immutability. Here, if he chose, Giovanni could trace his lineage back to ancient times.

By contrast, Giovanni's father's tomb was modest and unassuming. He had had built for himself, and his family, a small, square shaped building of only one storey, with a simple but elegantly carved entrance adorned with small windows on three sides. This was now Alessandro Lascorza's final resting place.

Kneeling on one knee at the side of the crypt and resting his forehead on the cold marble, Giovanni found himself in a contemplative mood, unable to find the appropriate words. After several moments of silence, he spoke softly. "The irony is not lost on me, Father. This is perhaps the most time we have spent together in some years." Pausing to find his next words, Giovanni took a deep breath and continued, "I have met with the Signoria.

There are storm clouds on the horizon. An unseen, unknown enemy lurking in the darkness. People speak openly of daemons in the shadows." He smiled weakly. "I suspect the reasoning is something rather more *earthly* in its origin..." hearing movement outside, Giovanni stopped though he quickly realised that it was the reassuring presence of Otto keeping watch but growing ever impatient to begin their journey.

Ignoring his aide, Giovanni whispered, "I have lent my support to this venture, for whatever good I can do. I have brought dishonour upon the family name; you may rest in peace that I do not intend for this to continue. I will regain our family honour. I will *fight* for Florence, Father." He leant forward, kissed the hand of the cold, marble effigy that his father had commissioned five years before and rose to his full height. Outside, he hardened his resolve and said, "I have made my peace, Otto. We must begin the preparations at once."

With a sage smile, Otto nodded. "I am glad that you have agreed to this, Giovanni. Through the coming hardship you will find salvation; through victory, you will find your redemption."

At that very moment, a little over thirty miles to the south, in the very heart of Siena itself, a young spy in the service of Florence watched the build-up of troops continue unabated. Assigned the codename *La Talpa* the spy slipped carefully through the small crowds, blending in with a practised ease. The mission was simply to observe and relay any useful information about Siena and her intentions. Ever since the spate of murders in

Florence had begun Siena had emerged as a credible threat. Mystery and intrigue hung in the very air in Siena. The situation in a city already notorious for the brutal oppression of its citizens had, in reality, become far, far worse over the succeeding weeks. Such was the feeling of desperation that the once content populace now lived in an environment of suspicion and mistrust. The threat of the authorities striking at any moment and hauling a nameless, faceless person into the decrepit, filthy dungeons for a perceived criminal act had become altogether too real for many families.

Sienese traders shouted to the passing throngs and a small formation of the city guard marched through the crowded streets of the merchant district, pushing and shoving any who came too near. The spy, who had until that moment been in a brief reverie, was aghast at the sheer number of troops and supplies being prepared, suddenly felt the gaze of the nearest guard.

"You there, what are you staring at? Come here! I'm talking to you!" shouted the nearest guard.

Absolutely sure that facing capture by the authorities and painful interrogation was not an option, La Talpa held the gaze of the approaching squad of soldiers just long enough, before casually changing direction and heading for a nearby side alley.

"Get back here you whore's child!" roared the guard.

Breaking into a run, the spy ignored the shout from behind and bolted as fast as possible, running down one street before turning left, then right, then left again into the literal maze of backstreets that was familiar only to locals.

Coming to a rest, La Talpa hid behind a partially collapsed wall, panting heavily, breathing heavily. Shedding items of clothing along the way, the spy had thrown them into nearby streets in an attempt to confuse the guards. This ploy had been to no avail for the guards were well-trained and drilled and had not lost the scent. The spy gripped the dagger hilt, knuckles white with the effort, and cursed having been flushed out so easily.

The guards walked closer towards the collapsed wall; they were almost within striking distance now and the spy's heart pounded. *Come on you bastards!* La Talpa thought as they made ready to leap out at the approaching men. Coiled like a snake waiting to strike, there was, at the last moment, a reprieve in the form of a shout in the near distance. The guards, hearing the shout, turned towards the sound and ran off as fast as they could.

Heaving a huge, but silent, sigh of relief whilst looking to the heavens, the spy decided that this was quite enough action for one day and began heading back to the inn.

In their private quarters, La Talpa began to remove outer garments, finally, slowly, pulling back the brown leather hood to reveal the face of a beautiful young woman. Olive-complexioned, with long flowing locks of dark hair, Isabella Maria de Franco, originally Venetian by birth, had been in the employ of the Signoria of Florence for several months now. A clever young woman of considerable charm, she had decided to seek her fame and fortune away from her father's silk trading business, much to his chagrin. It was during her first visit to Florence that her charms and abilities had first been brought to the attention of the acting Gonfaloniere of the time, who, in their infinite wisdom had found a useful position for her as a courtesan and spy, although this had been remarked upon as a most unusual move at the time.

It had been Isabella who had first alerted the authorities in Florence to the military build-up in Siena. It was she who had also reported the open and increasing hostility towards merchants and traders from Florence, signalling a cataclysmic change in attitude towards the on-going trade between the two cities. Deeply worried by these developments, the Signoria had seen fit to send Isabella into that accursed city to act as the eyes and ears of Florence and to try and infiltrate the inner circle of that accursed Tyrant of Siena, Pandolfo Petrucci.

Walking deeper into her chambers, she noticed that on her bed lay a sealed message. "What do we have here?" she said aloud. Quickly breaking open the seal, her eyes grew keen with interest as she read. She sat down on the bed trying to better make sense of the content of the message in her hand and to plan her next move; it was clear she hadn't a moment to lose.

Tuscan Hills, summer, 1483

Some days later, with his father interred in the family tomb, preparations for the coming journey were well underway. Giovanni and Otto sat in the Palazzo Lascorza and were deep in conversation. "Where do we even begin, Otto? An undertaking of this size...?"

"Simple," replied Otto. "We start with what we know. Preliminary investigations of the bodies of the men who were murdered a few weeks ago revealed that none of their fineries were taken and their money was left where it was. In short, nothing was taken that one would expect to be taken in a theft. We also know that all men were dispatched to the next life in a similar manner. Perhaps we should see if we can get a closer look at that last poor bastard. According to the information provided by the Signoria, I believe his name was Ferrante Uccello? I'd like to see what caused those wounds of his in particular,"

"Otto," replied Giovanni, "that man is either in the ground now or very close to being so; I doubt it'd be received too well with either his family or the authorities if we were to investigate his body for our own aims, even *with* the consent of the Signoria!"

"I agree, but there is something bigger at stake here. I say we need to consider all options," With a resigned expression on his face, Giovanni knew his aide was right. All the information they could get would help them in the longer run. "Then we need to get access to the body. How long will we need?"

"At most, just a few moments, Giovanni. I understand the body lies in a small chapel in the San Lorenzo district. If we can gain access to the chapel, I would like to look at the wounds in more detail. That might tell something about the murder weapon and perhaps, God willing, in turn help us to identify the murderer. If we can get to him, we may yet uncover the mystery here. You're looking pensive, why?"

Smiling, Giovanni replied simply, "Otto, old friend, I have an idea..,"

In the black of night, Giovanni and Otto crept through the sleeping streets of Florence, the occasional bark of a dog or yowl of cat their only companion. Coming upon the small, modest chapel in the San Lorenzo district, the two men stopped, hiding in a nearby doorway.

"There's a guard, so let me do the talking. I shall approach over there by the gated entrance and inform him that we are friends of the deceased and that we wish to pay our final respects. To sweeten the deal, I will give him a florin for his troubles. I will also inform him that we will be but a few moments with our friend to lessen his suspicions. Are we both clear as to the plan?"

"Yes, but what if he refuses? I brought my club to be on the safe side," continued the gruff Germanic mercenary grimly.

Raising his eyes to the heavens above and with a quiet sigh, Giovanni replied.

"Yes, if he refuses... you can club him. *Try* not to kill him though, please?" Otto shot him a pained look, followed by the briefest of smiles and then a short nod.

Moments later the two men ambled as nonchalantly as they could towards the guard closest to them, desperately hoping that they looked innocent and had every reason on earth to be there at that hour. The guard spotted them immediately and came to attention, the halberd at his side pointed menacingly at them. "Halt! Who goes there? Identify yourself!" he challenged.

"My name is Gotto Giambologna and this is my friend and colleague... Alfonso Bruni," replied Giovanni.

"We were the closest of friends of dear Ferrante Uccello who lies at rest within these very walls, *brothers* almost. We were away on business when this evil deed was done and so missed his brutal demise. We wish only to pay our last respects. Surely you can see your way to being kind enough to let us do so, Signor? We cannot let our brother go to his final resting place without first saying our farewells."

The guard looked from one man to the other; unsure of himself as if the entire situation were some form of test that he had to pass. Eventually, after summing up the situation in his mind, he spoke.

"You can go, but your friend," he said, pointing at Otto, "stays here, with me,"

Without even looking, Giovanni could sense Otto's eagerness, and turned to find him fingering his club with a wry, almost apologetic smile on his face.

"Signor," said Giovanni to the guard, handing over a florin, "perhaps this small donation will sweeten the situation? I'm sure you would find it most useful?"

Reluctantly, hesitating, whilst looking around the surrounding piazza, the guard nodded, lowered his halberd and ushered them through the small entrance set in the gate.

An audible sigh rang out in the silent darkness of the chapel. Allowing a moment for their eyes to adjust, Giovanni and Otto moved off towards the casket they could see at the far end of the north transept.

"Did you bring a light?" Otto whispered.

"Yes and I'm not lighting it until we're by the body. I don't want to arouse any further suspicion or attention."

With the greatest of care, both men walked with measured, quiet footsteps, neither man wanting to make any noise for fear of what that might bring.

After a moment of walking across the cold stone floor in pitch darkness, they came upon the casket. Carefully opening the lid fully, Giovanni lit the small lamp and they looked down at the pale, still form of Ferrante Uccello, the merchant who'd been murdered only days before.

Making the sign of the cross, Otto set to work, looking at the wounds whilst Giovanni looked on, keeping a vigilant eye on the rest of the chapel. If they were caught, the consequences would be serious, even *with* the consent of the Signoria.

"This man was garrotted," said Otto. "Look, this red line here across his throat, the same lines appear on his fingers. He struggled with his murderer trying to remove the garrotte from round his throat. Whoever did this… was good," he said admiringly. "We know cries were heard in the area during daylight hours. The murderer knew his victim, or at the very least he did from afar. He stalked his prey, found his moment and then pounced. In broad daylight, in a matter of moments, this man was dragged into that alleyway and slain."

Giovanni couldn't help but feel a pang of sympathy for the man laid out before him.

Forcibly opening the victim's mouth, Otto recoiled. "In the name of God above… This man's tongue has been cut out! Who'd do such a thing as this?"

"Perhaps, more importantly, *why* did they do this?" replied Giovanni in a whisper.

"Could it be symbolic, perhaps? A man without a tongue cannot easily talk," said Otto.

"It's a tenuous link at best. But if true, what was it that he had to be prevented from talking about? What did he know too much about? I don't think we will find any further answers here tonight. We should leave and continue our investigations in the surrounding area," said Giovanni.

"Wait," replied Otto, "there is one more place I've not checked!" Looking down at the soles of the dead man's boots, he noticed that they were still caked in dirt, or more specifically, silt and sand. "Signor, look at this. This is silt. It's either from the banks of a river, or… could it be sand, from a beach?"

Raising his hands in exasperation and scratching his head, Giovanni replied, "Otto, he was a merchant overseeing trade expeditions that would likely have required him to have been on or near trade ships. I have no idea what is happening here, but this is starting to concern me."

Otto shook his head slowly before replacing the lid of the casket, carefully and quietly. Not wanting to meet the guard again they located the nearest exit, crept silently out of the darkened chapel and hurried away into the night.

Republic of Florence, summer, 1483

The summer night's air was unexpectedly cold and a roaring log fire blazed in the bedchamber where Otto and Giovanni now sat.

Otto sat staring at the fire wistfully, smoking his pipe filled with angelikarot and blowing small smoke rings as he did so. Without warning, his voice broke the silence. "Many years ago, before I served your father, during my reckless youth, I saw service with a local militia in my native land. Not long after, I fought in my first battle. There were only a handful of survivors on each side. The slaughter was great, and I was bloodied, but otherwise unhurt." Otto paused for a moment. The smoke from his pipe formed curls in the firelight of the room. "Those of us who lived formed what effectively became a fellowship. A core of men tempered in the fires of battle who became almost as brothers. Our leader was a man of great savagery. He had a near unquenchable thirst for spilling blood. It mattered not to him who died, only that they did."

Giovanni sat in open-mouthed surprise at his aide's words.

Otto cleared his throat with an uncomfortable, dry cough before continuing. "I remember that icy, bitterly cold winter's morning in lower Swabia; we had received orders to move against a rebel stronghold known only to contain the old and weak, women and children. We were to punish them for the actions of their men folk, and punish them we did." His eyes welled up and glistened in the firelight. "Giovanni, you have

53

questioned my faith and, given your personal circumstances, I can hardly blame you. If you had witnessed what I have, if you had committed the atrocities that I have, perhaps you would believe differently."

Shaking his head, Giovanni replied, "What are you saying, Otto? What atrocities? What did you do?"

Otto sat, elbows on his knees, rubbing his hands over his swarthy face and drew a sharp intake of breath. "I killed the innocent, Giovanni. That is what I did. I killed the very people I have since sworn to protect my whole life. And for what higher purpose did I commit such slaughter? I did it for the money and glory, nothing else. However, I quickly learnt, to my everlasting shame, that there is no glory in taking life."

Wearing a thoughtful expression, Otto paused for breath. Taking a long drag on his pipe, he exhaled the smoke slowly. "Eventually, our leader grew increasingly deranged. For the rest of us, that terrible slaughter of innocent old men, women and children was a stain upon our personal honour, and yet for him, it was a sport. He revelled in the acts. He took personal delight in impaling his victims alive, even new born babies and children. His actions eventually led us to our doom. I believe his allegiance to us died the day he sold us out. His infamy had led to a censure upon our band. Claiming that we were rogues who no longer listened to his voice, he betrayed us and we were massacred at the Obere Burg castle in lower Swabia. I alone was fortunate enough to escape certain death for a second time and I have not seen that evil man since."

Giovanni, shaking his head more out of sympathy than horror spoke quietly. "Otto that was a long time ago. Whatever sins you have committed, you have more than paid for."

"More than twenty years have passed, but I have never forgotten his face. The devil himself is a less frightening prospect. I will never forget that man's eyes, or the sheer evil in them. Since that time, I have endured an unending personal crusade of penance to win back my honour and restore my name." The silence in the room was punctuated only by the spitting and crackling of the logs on the fire into which Otto continued to stare intently, lost in thought.

"Her name was Fabiana," said Giovanni suddenly in the orange, fire-lit darkness of the room. "She was a nun. Otto, you should have seen her. I have never been so moved by the beauty of another human being. She was so painfully beautiful and beguiling to me that, at times, I could not bring myself to look at her for fear of giving away the feelings in my heart. I loved her with such intent from the very moment I first laid eyes on her. Yet, I could not have her. She was a nun, devoted in her service to God. Or so I thought. We spoke only briefly, but it appeared that her heart belonged not just to God, but to another man also. Even though I thought she was devoted to God, and it is now evident that she wasn't, she still loved another man more than me."

Otto turned from the fire at the sound of pain and despair in Giovanni's voice. With a weak smile and a brief snort, Giovanni continued, "Some months later, she bore his child. It was the shame of being found out that led her to take her own life." Giovanni fell silent, nodding as though in agreement with some internal dialogue running through his mind. "She threw herself from the roof of the nunnery of San Pier Maggiore and the most beautiful and amazing creature I have ever set eyes upon was gone from this world. Denied a proper, decent burial, her body was taken to the outskirts of the city and dumped at the crossroads to the east. I have no place in my heart for any organisation, Otto, any God, or anything that has such little compassion and so much disdain for the most vulnerable amongst us."

Otto stood from his seat by the fire and reached out to Giovanni, touching him on the arm. "God is there for us all, Giovanni, even when you least expect it. His hand has guided me many a time on the field of battle. It is a good thing that you have agreed to do. Service to your city and the defence of those unable to defend themselves is a noble thing; I think He guides you now. Find yourself through this venture. Find and redeem yourself."

Giovanni turned and stared from the window of his bed chamber, while Otto returned to his chair by the fireplace, packing and re-lighting his pipe. Rubbing his bearded chin, and with a soft, faraway voice Giovanni spoke.

"I think it would be prudent if our investigations continued in Siena; there appears to be little more that we can discover here."

With a shrug and a typical, beaming smile, Otto replied, "That won't be an easy course of action though I think there is wisdom in that. When do we leave?"

"As soon as possible, I think. There is little time to lose, but we should inform the Signoria of our intentions. They won't look too kindly upon us if we merely vanished without leaving some indication of what we were doing or where we were going. Besides which, we may well need their assistance at some juncture in time."

Slapping the young Giovanni on the side of his arm, Otto announced with a grin, "Your father would be proud, young Master! I will send a messenger who will carry word of our intentions to them at first light. For now, we should rest; there will be a long, dangerous road ahead of us."

The next morning preparations for their journey were underway; the household servants made the necessary arrangements, packing food and supplies onto the horses, whilst Otto prepared the bridles. Giovanni had changed from his usual finery into less conspicuous attire of a plain brown doublet and leather britches. Although less refined, being thicker, the fabric of his jacket afforded more protection from light weapons and the elements. Otto, too, had removed his rather obvious doublet with the heraldic arms of Florence and changed into an altogether simpler set of garments, not unlike that of Giovanni. Both men desired to remain incognito as neither knew how they would be received in Siena. Nor did either man wish to prejudice their investigations there.

The returning messenger called out across the internal courtyard of the Palazzo Lascorza. He was clearly out of breath and had made every effort to cross Florence as swiftly as possible. Bowing low to Giovanni, the messenger caught his breath before speaking. "My Lord Lascorza, Signor Lascorza! Your message has been delivered to the Signoria as requested. They asked me to give you this in return."

Replying with a smile and taking the sealed message from the other man, Giovanni nodded his head briefly in thanks before breaking open the red wax seal on the scroll and reading the message. "Excellent news. I thank you for your efforts."

Letting out a loud whistle to his companion, Giovanni signalled that it was time to leave. Both men climbed into the saddles of their respective horses. The gates to the palazzo were opened, and out they rode into the streets of Florence.

Leaning over to Giovanni, Otto remarked, "We should leave via the eastern gate, then perhaps take the southern road straight to Siena. No distractions; we proceed directly there."

"Agreed. We should make for Siena with all possible speed, but it's still a good several days' ride. The terrain will slow us down considerably. We still ought to find some place to rest and shelter to be fully prepared for what lies ahead," replied the young Lascorza.

Walking their horses through the busy streets of Florence, both men had chance to reflect on the journey ahead, and not for the first time did Giovanni wonder at the true nature of what was happening to his beloved city and what manner of evil forces were arrayed against them. He suppressed a pang of envy of the masses around him going about their everyday lives. A small, but significant part of him wished to be doing anything but this, anything but walking willingly into the lion's den. Yet an even greater part of him couldn't help but feel excited about the adventure ahead.

They at last reached the outer walls of the city and finally the eastern gate. Here, vast and imposing, the walls towered above the nearest buildings and both men looked up at the enormous gatehouse, wondering when, or even if, they would see their city again. A huge grin spread over the grizzled, veteran face of Otto as they rode through the gate, and he saw the promise of adventure that lay ahead.

"Ah, the open road, there is nothing better!" said Otto.

The younger Lascorza could not help but be inspired by his companion's infectious enthusiasm and allowed himself a wry smile and a quick look back at the full majesty of Florence fading slowly into the distance behind them.

Siena, summer, 1483

Giacomo Bugiardini was a well-connected man of Siena, a principled, handsome man possessed of aquiline features and a calm manner. Although he was wealthy, he was a kind-hearted soul who wished for nothing more than prosperity to return to his city. Bugiardini longed to see his children reach adulthood and for him to grow old along with his beautiful wife. Despite his wealth and resources, he dressed moderately for he was a pious and devout man and his morals were utterly beyond reproach.

Though only in his early thirties, Giacomo Bugiardini's stature had grown in the administration prior to Pandolfo Petrucci's meteoric rise to power. His opposition to Petrucci had been duly noted and had marked him out as a dangerous man, a verified trouble maker. As yet though, the tyrant was not able to eliminate him, for Bugiardini was an immensely popular man with the masses. And yet, if Petrucci could not eliminate Bugiardini, those close to him surely could.

Bugiardini shared a beautiful, warm home in the centre of Siena with his wife and two young daughters. The sound of children's laughter emanated from the courtyard. Smiling, Giacomo Bugiardini walked out into the brilliant sunshine to where his daughters were playing and to where his wife, Amelia, and the household servants were keeping careful watch over them. The main entrance to the palazzo was guarded, as was the case with the homes of many prominent figures of the city.

Giacomo caught his wife's attention and sauntered over to her, kissing her tenderly on her cheek as she held him tightly.

"How was the assembly?" she asked.

"The same as ever. They pander to Petrucci's every dangerous whim, whilst ignoring the needs of the people," Giacomo sighed.

"I meant," replied Amelia, "how was he with you? It concerns me that your opposition to him marks us out for retribution. He is not to be trusted. He is far too dangerous."

"Ah, my darling Amelia, you are wise enough for both of us, I think. He *is* dangerous, but he also knows that my family is popular with the people and supported in various places outside of Siena. He would not dare strike against me. He knows the uproar it would cause and the support he would lose. Relax, my love. We must steer the course and take our stand against tyranny. If we do not, who will?"

"I hope you are right," she replied, "because fear is rife in this city now. It walks the streets, preying on the weak and innocent. All are susceptible to it, including us. I do not fear for us, but I do fear for them," Amelia continued, gesturing discreetly towards their two young girls. A cold chill ran through Giacomo. He was not entirely blind to the risks involved with providing opposition to Petrucci.

Turning back to his wife, he nodded and said, "I will be as careful as I can, but we must all remain vigilant." With that, Giacomo walked over to the guards to confer with them about matters of security before leaving on a secret errand.

Giacomo walked casually through the cobbled streets of Siena, his wife and children safely in the hands of his household guard. He had arranged to meet with an important person. He had recently been made aware of an informant working for Florence who would be able to assist him in his desire to remove Petrucci from power and return his city to a more stable state of affairs.

Making his way through the crowded streets, he spied his destination -- a free house where travellers could stay and rest whilst conducting their business. It also doubled as an inn. He knew the owners and trusted them implicitly. Upon entering the free house, Giacomo smelled the heavy scent of roasted pig mingled with the ale that was served there. The background noise of chattering people was all that greeted his ears; no-one seemed to pay him any significant attention when he entered.

As he scanned the crowded room, he made eye contact with the owner of the establishment and walked over to greet him. "Piero," he said.

"Giacomo, good to see you old friend," replied the bartender.

"Is my contact here?"

"She is indeed, Signor. She is seated over in the corner,"

With raised eyebrows, Giacomo replied, *"She*? She is over where?" The bartender pointed to the far corner where a table carefully positioned allowed the best view of the room and its occupants. Giacomo nodded his thanks and turned round and walked over to the figure in the corner. Eyeing his surroundings, he made a coughing noise to attract the attention of the young woman sitting at the table in front of him.

A beautiful, olive-skinned woman with intelligent and alert brown eyes and long, flowing dark hair looked up at him. "Can I help you?" she said.

"My name is Giacomo Bugiardini; I believe you were expecting me. Is there somewhere we can talk in private?"

Nodding, she gestured towards the stairs. "We can go to my room; we should find the privacy we need to talk there."

Returning to the bar, Giacomo watched as the woman picked up her drink and headed for the stairs. A few minutes later and at the top of the stairs, he walked the length of the small corridor before knocking on the door and entering the young woman's room. Under normal circumstances this would have been considered scandalous at the very least, but they'd both been so circumspect that they'd managed to leave the bar without anyone noticing.

Upon entering the young woman's room, he checked for intruders and then searched behind drapes and wall hangings to ensure that there were no concealed listening holes. Once satisfied, both of them sat down opposite each other.

"I believe you have me at a disadvantage my lady. I have introduced myself, but you have not returned the courtesy. Of whom do I have the honour of addressing?"

"That is not important now, though you may call me Isabella," she replied. "What is more important is what I'm about to tell you. Florence suspects that Siena is in some way implicated in a spate of murders that occurred there recently. If true, this behaviour will not be tolerated. Agents are to be dispatched by the Signoria to get to the bottom of the web of lies and deceit here. It would be prudent if you could meet and liaise with them. To my knowledge, they are faithful servants of Florence who bear no ill-will against Siena. It appears that they have the same aim as you."

Shrugging his shoulders, Giacomo replied, "Of course, I am in their service. What are their names? How will I recognise them?"

"Leave that to me," replied Isabella. "I shall make initial contact with them, and when possible, lead them to you. It is no secret that you are a man of resource and that your opposition to Petrucci is vehement in its nature. If that is true, then I fear for your safety and that of your family."

A resigned frown on Giacomo's face confirmed that he was well aware of the potential dangers. "I have heard this before, I think," he said, recalling the conversation he had had with his wife, not half an hour before. "When will they arrive in Siena? In fact, how will they even get past the city guard?" he continued.

"I am assured that they will have a plan for that. We do not need to be concerned. It is up to us to ensure that they are safe and taken care of until we can get to the heart of this. Can we count on you? Will you pledge your support to our and Siena's cause?"

"Yes of course, I have already stated that I would assist you."

"You have, but you must be absolutely certain of this. There can be no middle ground here. What we are working towards could be counted as treason. You must steel your heart for the days and weeks ahead. I'm sure I need not remind you of the consequences should we be caught. Pandolfo Petrucci will show absolutely no mercy."

"My lady, may I remind you," replied Giacomo, "that I have more than most to lose. I have no fear for myself, only for my wife and children. I would be," he paused momentarily, "heartbroken if anything were to happen to them. Besides, I believe we are resolved in this. They will make their entry to the city, you will locate them, bring them to me, and I shall provide whatever assistance and support they require to ensure that Petrucci is removed one way or another."

Nodding, Isabella replied, "Wait for my signal. We shall meet again soon." With a low bow, Giacomo took his leave.

Moments later, a strange, worried sensation, passed over Giacomo as he walked the short distance back to his home. Feeling as though he were being watched, the hairs rose on the back of his neck. Slowing his pace, he turned round to look behind him. Seeing nothing of any note, he turned to carry on walking, yet his instincts screamed at him that something was very wrong. The streets were quiet, too quiet as no dogs barked and no children played. Even the traders seemed quieter in their activities than usual.

Breathing heavily and with a grimace, Giacomo started to run, slowly at first, then as the feeling persisted, he ran harder and faster than he ever had in his life. Reaching the entrance to his house, he hammered at the doors demanding access. Nothing happened. The guards who would normally have opened up in seconds were nowhere to be seen.

A sick thrill of fear pierced him now as he began to slam his shoulder into the gates. The doors were too solid, however, and repelled his attempts. Walking rapidly down the street adjacent to his house, he noticed that the door to the courtyard was slightly ajar. Adrenaline surged through his veins. With one fluid motion, he drew his sword and held it poised at the ready before pushing open the door.

Before him in the courtyard, he was greeted by a scene of utter carnage. His servants had all been slaughtered, run through like animals, their warm bodies pooling blood around them, but of his wife and daughters there was no sign. The guards that had watched over his home, men that he had trusted with the lives of his wife and children, that he had served with, were nowhere to be found.

Walking as deliberately as he could manage, he headed towards the entrance to his home, a feeling of nausea coursing through every fibre of his being, nerves screaming a warning. Pausing upon the threshold, he was greeted by the most horrific sight a man could ever see. The bodies of his wife and children lay in a crumpled heap on the ground a few feet in front of him; their throats slit from ear to ear, mouths agape and their tongues brutally cut out. Giacomo doubled over and vomited on the spot.

Tearing at his hair he sobbed loudly and uncontrollably, keening and wailing and crying out his beloveds' names all the while. His agonising cries were heard from outside his home where passers-by gathered in dismay at his plight and terrible distress. Alerted by a runner, it was not long before Giacomo's friends arrived.

Many hours later, when the necessary clearing up had been carried out and the bodies of his wife and children had been washed, dressed and laid together on trestles, Giacomo tried to piece together the events of the terrible day in his mind. His eyes were bleary from weeping, his throat ragged and sore with emotion. His voice cracked as he spoke, "I know the devil that is responsible for this evil act, and his life, in one way or another, is now forfeit. My wife and children have paid the price for my refusal to bow down to this man. Today, I vow to end the tyranny that lies at the heart of this city."

With red raw eyes and a tight knot of searing pain and misery in his chest, Giacomo gritted his teeth and sat with his fists tightly clenched in the courtyard of his home. He looked up at the darkening sky. Mingled now with his grief was an intense and deadly anger. If it were done with his very last breath, Giacomo would avenge his wife and children.

Tuscany, summer, 1483

The following morning, the rolling Tuscan countryside swept past Giovanni and Otto as they pushed ahead on the road to Siena.

After many hours of riding, both men were tired, in need of refreshment and their mounts hung their heads in sheer exhaustion. Spotting a small forest ahead, both men agreed it would be a prudent course of action to take rest and to plan exactly what would happen when they reached Siena.

As dusk approached, Giovanni and Otto sat round a crackling fire. Otto had caught a small, wild boar and was roasting it on a spit. "We should be careful when we enter Siena," he said. "It's a lair of thieves, liars and murderers. Of that I am certain."

Picking up a juicy leg of boar, Giovanni mulled over what his friend was saying. "I do not think most of them are so different from us, Otto," he mused. "I understand they live under a tyrant, a brutal man with no sense of moral decency, a man for whom fairness and righteousness are impossible to know; a vile, vicious and cruel man. Those poor denizens of that city have my pity, not my hatred. Not for them the republican ideals by which we are fortunate enough to be ruled.

"That may be so, young Signor, but either way, there are those who would wish us a tremendous amount of ill-will whilst we are there, for Florence has many enemies, chief amongst them, the city of Siena. Ultimately, it is within the nature of us, and the duty of every freeborn man, woman and child to rally against tyranny wherever and whenever it is found, for those who live a life of involuntary servitude cannot be said to be living at all. It is to live a just life of honour and service beholden to a greater good that we must strive for."

Giovanni, recognising his own late father's words, allowed a knowing smile to spread across his face. "They may not be too different from us, but they have all too readily accepted their fate. They do not yet rally against it, and for that, I cannot but hold them in contempt," Otto continued. For a moment, both men were silent.

Changing the subject Otto broke the silence first, "It is reasonable that, as the men who were murdered were merchants, we should start in the merchants' quarters… conduct our investigations as carefully as we might reasonably be expected to do. It is imperative that we do not draw attention to ourselves. It might help if we knew what these men were trading in, too."

"Well, indeed," replied Giovanni. "Before any of that, though, we'll need to make entry into the city itself. We're not dressed as merchants or traders, and we have nothing to trade, so they'll most likely bar entry to us."

"Yes, that is a good point," considered Otto, rubbing his beard. "We would need disguises I think." A huge smile creased the old aide's face, "I have an idea about that."

Looking puzzled Giovanni replied, "Well, if you can get us in, we'll still need accommodation before we begin the investigation. With a stroke of luck, we may uncover what it was that was so terrible that their lives were taken in order to prevent them from talking."

Unbeknownst to them, in the undergrowth less than twenty feet away lurked a deadly threat. Otto heard the distinctive noise of a twig breaking. "To arms!" he roared leaping up and hefting his mighty two-handed sword.

Giovanni swung round, his lighter, smaller blade held before him. In response, five men leapt from the bushes at the same time and several arrows narrowly missed their mark. A clash of steel ensued and the sound of sword meeting sword rang loud through the clearing. Otto parried a thrust aimed for his throat and responded by kicking his opponent's legs out from under him. With a grunt Otto raised his sword above his head and stabbed it down into the prone man's chest. A gurgling scream that died in his opponent's throat signalled that the man was dead.

Otto desperately looked over at Giovanni to see him fending off two men as best he could. Parrying a wicked slash from his nearest foe, Giovanni grabbed his would-be killer's arm before promptly head-butting him in the face and was rewarded with the satisfying crunch of broken bone. Dropping to his knees in pain, the man clutched at his face trying to stem the blood; Giovanni swiftly and without mercy dispatched him by running him through. That left three men. Three men that they knew of, out in the open, if indeed there were any more still in the thick forest that surrounded them. Giovanni smiled and bowed to his attackers with a flourish, "Gentlemen, now that we're fully acquainted, who's next?" The three surviving attackers glanced briefly at each other before rushing forward in unison, their swords raised, and each screaming a bloodcurdling battle cry.

Moments later, their assailants dead, Giovanni and Otto were left panting, clutching their sides as they fought, this time, to regain their breath. Escaping serious injury, they were cut and bloodied with minor wounds, "Who…were they?" panted Giovanni.

"I suspect our departure from Florence did not go unnoticed. Either that or they were outlaws. They certainly weren't professional killers or we would be lying dead in their place. The lands between Florence and Siena are prone to such acts. If they were in the employ of Siena, we may find it more difficult to gain entry to the city as they will already know that we are coming and will be watching for us," replied Otto.

For once, Giovanni smiled first. With a twinkle in his eye said, "An entire city against the two of us? I don't like their odds."

Otto shook his head in mild disbelief, wiped his sword clean and re-sheathed it. In a matter of minutes, both men had gathered up their belongings, doused the fire, re-loaded the horses and were continuing wearily on their way. The forest soon gave way once more to the rolling hills and farmland that the region was famous for. After a while, with only the sound of the horses' hooves trotting on the dusty track, Giovanni spoke, "I ought to have mentioned this sooner, but I could not be certain that we weren't being followed. We are to meet up with a contact within Siena, but that still leaves the problem of getting past the main gate. I received word of this when our messenger to the Signoria returned to us; our contact appears to be female."

"A woman?" Otto remarked, his eyebrows raised in surprise.

"Yes; and by all accounts a highly accomplished and daring one at that! Her name is given only as Isabella," said Giovanni. "We're to meet with her as soon as we gain entry to the city. What help or use she'll be to us at this stage, I cannot tell."

"Pray tell, why have you only divulged this now?" said Otto.

"I told you, I had a suspicion we were being followed or watched as we travelled. I did not wish to give any information away about our contact. It appears much hinges on her. If we can gain entry to the city and meet up with her, my hope is that she will have sufficient influence to enable her to introduce us into the inner circle of the ruling council."

As the two men continued riding, the warm summer sun finally set, casting deep shadows all around them as the sky cloaked itself in hues of purple and crimson and the intense heat of the day faded to the cool of the night. Some distance later they came upon a small inn conveniently located at the side of the road. After seeing first to their horses, both men settled down for a night of planning and rest.

The following morning, having eaten a hearty breakfast of bread, salted meats and eggs washed down with fresh water, they paid the innkeeper their dues, then set off on the final straight for Siena.

Spotting what he was looking for in the distance, Otto began to outline his plan to gain entry into the city. "There, that trade caravan; do you see it, over there in the distance?"

"Yes, I see it," replied the younger man. "One can only presume your intention is for us to somehow take our place within it and thus smuggle ourselves through the gates and into the city at large?"

"Quite, if my plan works, we could... no wait," he paused, "I have an even better idea!" Otto's gaze turned from the trade caravan, to a small group coming from a different direction altogether. "There! There is our ticket into Siena," said Otto confidently. With a quizzical look, Giovanni glanced to where Otto was pointing.

"What? I don't see anything besides a small group of people. I think the trade caravan would be a better bet."

"You have not heard of the Commedia dell Arte, Signor?" replied Otto.

"Of course, but how can you tell it is they from this distance?"

"I had the pleasure of seeing a troupe once. They were magnificent! I'd recognise their kind anywhere," said the older man. "If we play it just right, and perhaps explain to them that we intend to play a prank on a senior noble within Siena, it might appeal to their capricious nature. You wait here. Leave it to me. I shall return presently." And with that, Otto spurred his horse and rode over to where the Commedia dell Arte troupe was making its preparations to enter Siena.

In reality a mere half an hour had elapsed, yet to Giovanni, it had seemed like a good day's worth of waiting. Eventually, smiling, Otto returned to his new master holding a package. "It took a little persuasion, but eventually they agreed to let us join their troupe, albeit temporarily. However, there was one condition," he said.

Giovanni shook his head and replied, "What is it? What condition have they laid upon us?"

"Mmm, well, it's more a condition upon you, my lord," replied Otto with as serious a face as he could manage. "They have seen you from afar, your physique, your figure, age, and, with not a little encouragement from me… well, there is no easy way for me to say this. They believe you would be perfect to play the part of Harlequin. In order to do so, they would require you to wear this."

Looking down at the multi-coloured, multi-patterned suit, Giovanni threw his head back and replied with a deep belly laugh, before realising that Otto was being entirely serious. "Surely you jest, Otto?" was all that Giovanni could splutter in response.

Moments later, both men were galloping towards the troupe of performing artists and actors, with the younger man still holding the unusual package of clothing whilst shooting the older man a look of reproach. Approaching the camp, they were greeted with smiles and shouts of joy and welcome from the troupe of performers. With both men having dismounted, Otto introduced Giovanni to the troupe. "My lord, these people have kindly agreed to aid us in our japes and high jinks! Meet Piero who plays the part of Pantalone, Giocomo the wisest, and perhaps some might say the *elder* within the group," said Otto winking at the portly Giocomo. "He plays the role of Il Dottore," Otto finished the introductions before explaining in more detail to the assembled troupe of performers what he had in mind.

"It is our intention to play a high jape upon a certain nobleman, who shall remain unnamed!" laughed Otto. "He is a dear friend of ours and would appreciate the efforts we have gone to, but first, we must enter Siena unrecognised, for all surprise would be lost if my companion and I were to be discovered before we had chance to play our prank. You would of course, receive our warmest thanks and pecuniary reimbursement for your troubles," Otto finished his brief speech with a bow and a flourish, while the troupe cheered and clapped their hands in approval and made their final preparations for entering Siena by getting into their characters and costumes at once.

"If I am to be Harlequin, who might you be playing, my dear Otto?" asked Giovanni innocently.

"Ha!" replied Otto. "I am a man of many faces Signor Lascorza. I am to be a fire-breather!"

"A fire-breather eh? Good for you,"

"Yes. It will help if I drink much ale first, to line my gullet you understand," said Otto with a grin that spread across his face.

"Oh, of *course*," replied Giovanni sarcastically.

Within the hour, all makeup and costume had been applied, the troupe had assembled and the final march to Siena had begun. Appearing from his tent in his brightly coloured costume and with his face covered in a mask as black as onyx, Giovanni looked as though he'd been born for the part, much to the amusement of his older companion.

"Don't say a word, Otto. Just don't. Think better of it; I will hear no words, I warn you!" the young Florentine snapped.

Stifling a laugh, still smiling, Otto raised his hands in appeasement. "Not a word," said Otto, placing his right hand over his heart. "You have my word as a man of honour. Anyway, to business, we are presently headed for the northern gate. You said our contact will meet us immediately inside the gates. How, pray tell, are we to recognise her?"

Still itching and feeling very foolish inside his new attire, Giovanni replied awkwardly, "She will be clad in a long, flowing dress of crimson and white, the very colours of the heraldic coat of arms of Florence. She will be positioned somewhere prominent, so we must be on the lookout for her."

Otto mulled this over before replying, "And does she know what to look for in us?"

"Well, I highly doubt she'll be looking for an idiot dressed as a court jester and a fire-breathing ape half out of his face on ale, if that's what you're referring to!" snapped Giovanni peevishly.

With a look of wounded pride, Otto remembering his place, bit back a retort and added, "So we must find a way of signalling to her our presence, and then find a way to rendezvous with her."

A smug smile lit Giovanni's face. "Leave that to me," he replied.

Looming ahead of them in the distance lay Siena, its enormous walls growing ever larger as they drew closer to the city. The road entering the city became ever more congested due solely to the fact that the city guard was paying close attention to everyone who entered. Giovanni tapped Otto on the arm, nodding in the direction of the trade caravan that they had originally intended to infiltrate. "Notice the guards are paying particular attention to it. There is little chance we would have remained undetected," whispered Giovanni. A casual nod of Otto's head was his only reply.

The city guard had indeed paid very close attention to the traders, partly for opportunities for bribery and in part because they were under strict orders to root out any potential spies trying to gain access to the city. The heavily armed and armoured men searched through the traders' carts, pulling back tarpaulins to reveal the goods that lay beneath, checking the underside of the carriages and searching the men and women that made up the traders themselves.

Arriving at the enormous, iron-studded gates, both Giovanni and Otto fell into their new characters as ably as they could. Riding on the back of a rickety old cart, Otto blew fire from his mouth with the skill and panache of one who had been doing so for years, whilst Giovanni, by sheer chance, excelled himself with his rendition of the

Harlequin. The gathered crowd roared, clapping and cheering as they showed their approval. Looking up as they passed through the great gates, Giovanni breathed an internal sigh of relief. They had arrived in Siena at long last.

Siena, summer, 1483

With a beautiful flowing dress of the finest crimson and white silk damasque, Isabella moved through the crowds with a feline grace. Where she walked, men looked, stood and gawped at her beauty, wondering where her chaperone was. Approaching the northern gate, her attention was immediately drawn to the large crowd that had gathered there. Frowning, she entered the throng, hoping to take up a position that would enable her to be recognised by the two men she was to meet. She looked around and saw nothing out of the ordinary save for the Commedia dell Arte troupe that was starting to enter the gates surrounded by a laughing crowd.

Working her way to the most prominent position she could find, she stood and waited, her eyes constantly scanning the crowd. Moments later, the carts carrying the travelling troupe of performers drew nearer to her, so near in fact that a young man in a Harlequin costume was able to make eye contact with her. He was supple, lithe, with a well-defined physique that did him great service. To her astonishment, he leapt off the cart, grabbed her by the waist and swept her back onto the cart in one easy, seemingly practised movement. Thinking that this was all part of the act, the crowd cheered even louder.

"Unhand me you savage!" exclaimed Isabella, lashing out with her right hand.

Grabbing her wrist and leaning closer, Giovanni whispered in her ear, "Isabella I presume? My name is Giovanni Lascorza; I am here with my personal aide and good friend, Otto Baldwinson. We were sent by the

Signoria of Florence to meet with you. Now, before you give us all away, sing, dance, make merry and pretend that this was intended lest the crowd turn nasty and try to save you!"

Realising that she had little choice and that these were her intended contacts, she immediately smiled and danced a merry jig on top of the cart to the raucous amusement of the onlookers.

A short while later, having passed through the gates and outer walls of Siena the troupe made its way to the centre of Siena via one of the main arterial routes. Once the crowd had abated, the troupe settled into its holding area in the market near the Piazza Del Campo and began preparations for that evening's performance.

Distancing themselves from the rest of the troupe, Giovanni and Otto found a secluded side street and, along with Isabella introduced themselves formally. With the formalities out of the way, Isabella asked the first question. "What have your investigations revealed in Florence?"

Both men glanced at each other before Giovanni replied. "We had chance to inspect one of the murdered merchants. It seems he was garrotted shortly before his tongue was cut out. None of his fineries were taken, his purse was supposedly full to the brim with florins and it was an act carried out in broad daylight with virtually no witnesses. The only ones who did hear something attributed it to what they thought were drunks fighting. In short, it was carried out by someone with consummate skill. Otto and I believe the killing was symbolic in its nature, for all three of the merchants that were murdered were killed in this way and all three of them had previously visited Siena. Simply put, they knew too much. Exactly what it was they knew too much about, we're here to find out."

Nodding, Isabella replied, "I have observed a huge increase in troop numbers, their disposition, and their supplies, munitions, everything. The entire city feels on a knife edge. I have witnessed countless arrests of alleged subversives, although in reality this term applies to any and all that the great tyrant himself takes a dislike to."

"Pandolfo Petrucci?" murmured Otto.

"Correct. Little, if anything, happens in Siena without his say. He's a man of great evil and limitless cunning. He is rumoured to be on good terms with the Borgias of all people. His stock knows no earthly bounds. Although I have no proof yet, I can't help but feel this man has something in mind for Florence, although again, quite why, or what I do not know, either."

"Then it is up to us to find out," replied Giovanni curtly. "Come, we must hurry back to the troupe, or they may grow suspicious."

"Ah, dearest friends," said Piero. "We had begun to wonder where you had gone to."

"Merely seeing the sights my friend," replied Otto with as congenial a smile as he could manage. "We are not familiar with Siena despite our noble friend upon whom we intend to play the prank having lived here for a number of years now." With his hand to his mouth, he whispered in a hushed tone, "Besides, I rather think our young friends," motioning towards Giovanni and Isabella, "have much in common and wished to," he paused for effect, "get to know each other better. Naturally I acted as their chaperone," he chuckled, finishing with a wink. Piero nodded and looked over at the younger pair and smiled knowingly.

Oblivious to the conversation Otto was having on his behalf, Giovanni began to look around him in greater detail. Although he could not help but compare its magnificence with that of Florence, he busied himself with noting all the possible escape routes should the situation demand it.

Isabella stood beside him realising immediately what he was doing. "Should things turn sour," she remarked, "you must follow me and do exactly as I say, without me, both of you stand almost no chance of escaping this city alive. Do you understand?" Turning to her in agreement, Giovanni was, momentarily nonplussed by her beauty. He blushed in response, hoping that Isabella would not be able to see his countenance clearly in the dimming light of the close of day.

The troupe was busying itself for its first performance in Siena. The warmth of the day had begun to fade a little, and, as the sun began to set, lights were being lit all around the city. In the Piazza Del Campo where the troupe was due to perform, the day's activities had started to wind down and in their place more people began to gather, waiting expectantly. A quiet murmur could be heard, and the excitement was almost tangible.

Realising that he was almost entirely ignorant of his acting role, Giovanni had seen fit to take some tuition from one of the troupe members. With little time to practise, his nerves were as great as Otto's ale consumption. Sipping on his friend's ale, Giovanni began to prepare himself for the coming performance. By now, the sun had set fully, the crowd had swelled to epic proportions and the performance was only moments away. The Piazza Del Campo was brightly illuminated by dozens of lanterns. In the middle distance, a small enclave of people had gathered with the best view of the impromptu stage that had been erected.

Isabella surreptitiously leaned into Giovanni and Otto motioning towards the gathered group. "Petrucci!" she hissed. "And look," she added the invective, "he's surrounded by his cronies – sycophants, cowards and *murderers* all. A more evil, villainous collection of men you will be hard pressed to find anywhere in northern Italy. As for Petrucci, he is rivalled only by the Borgia for his degeneracy and corruption. He tolerates no opposition; all who stand in his way are disposed of without question. He is feared by the populace, his rule is absolute, and his mercy non-existent. I would wager all that I am on him being behind the unrest and strife in Florence in some form or other. His heart truly is the dark heart of a daemon."

Horrified by the import of what Isabella had just said, Giovanni, unwittingly gazed at Petrucci and even from this distance, his very presence sent a shudder through his soul. "What are you doing?" hissed Isabella nudging Giovanni. "Stop staring at him. Do you want the *entire* city guard bearing down on us?"

Jolted back into reality, Giovanni collected himself, looked back at her, holding his hand over his heart, "Of course not. Now, let's make this performance one to remember."

Otto, meanwhile, having continued ingratiating himself with the ale, was somewhat red in the face. Giovanni, dressed in his white suit emblazoned with multi-coloured diamonds, shot him a disappointed look and shook his head.

With the performance under way, the crowd made their pleasure known through cries of laughter, loud boos and shouts. Otto added to the theatrical thrill by periodically managing to do a half decent job of fire-breathing or eating, amazing the crowd and generally playing the fool. Giovanni, sensing that he was getting into his stride, began to enjoy himself. With a whirl and a flourish, with a twist and a turn, he performed his role as though he'd always been an actor, but it was not to last.

Roughly half way through the troupe's performance, events took a turn for the worse as Otto slipped from the edge of the stage grabbing hold of Giovanni as he did so. Falling into the crowd had de-masked both men, much to the amusement of Otto and the chagrin of Giovanni. The crowd, thinking that this was all part of the show, roared their approval and pushed them back onto the stage before the two performers had time to cover their faces. Otto, bare faced and with a beaming grin, bowed to the crowd whilst Giovanni struggled to replace both his mask and Otto's.

"Put your damn mask on you clumsy old oaf. You'll see us both killed!" Giovanni bellowed over the din of the crowd.

Struggling to focus, Otto suddenly realised the gravity of the situation, "Forgive me, Signor!" he replied, but it was too late.

Over in the middle distance, a tall, dark-skinned man standing to the right of Petrucci whispered in the tyrant's ear. Seconds later, screams erupted from the crowd surrounding the stage as from every direction, heavily armed soldiers emerged.

"I want them alive!" came a shout from the small group in the centre of the crowd.

Even in his inebriated state, the jolt of adrenaline brought about by the recognition of a face in the crowd made Otto's blood run cold. His eyes, still befuddled with drink, tried desperately to focus on the face as it blurred in and out of his vision. There, in the small group gathered round Petrucci stood a man whose face was dredged from the dark, depths of Otto's memories.

Swaying from side to side now, Otto rubbed his eyes, before raising his right hand to shield them from the glare of the lantern. A flashing glint from the sword of the nearest city guard caught his eye. Otto lashed out with his fire stick catching the unfortunate man in the face and causing him to cry out in pain. With a sharp intake of breath and a puzzled look on his face, Otto mumbled, "What are they doing here?"

"They're here for us," shouted Giovanni. "Get moving!" Frantically, Giovanni began to hunt around for a weapon, but both his and Otto's swords were packed away in the wagons. Grabbing one of Otto's still burning, fire-eating sticks, Giovanni began waving his makeshift weapon around with a vengeance. He thrust the red hot stick at the nearest guardsman catching him full in the face. The latter, spurred on by his comrades, had made the mistake of getting too close; he reeled back, his hair burning and his eyes ruined.

Otto, meanwhile, breathed fire over the nearest group of guards who promptly ran screaming in terror. Throwing back his head with laughter, he failed to notice the rope that snaked round his legs. With one quick tug of the rope, he fell with a heavy thud, landing, winded, flat on his back. Now surrounded, half a dozen heavily armoured city guards pointed their halberds at his prone form.

Giovanni surrendered the flaming torch, placing it on the ground, before raising his hands in the air. Knowing that Otto's life depended on his actions, he stood over his fallen banner man, and begged the soldiers that threatened them, for clemency.

The crowd, for the most part had dispersed screaming in terror lest they became caught up in the melee. Those remaining parted as Pandolfo Petrucci and his entourage walked, carefully, gracefully yet in a manner that hinted of malicious intent, towards the stage. Their footsteps on the cobblestones rang out in the deafening silence.

From the entourage, stepped a physically unremarkable man in his early thirties, a man however, for whom the fates had gifted an intelligent face combined with a piercing gaze that few men could hold. What he lacked in physical presence, he more than made up for in his terrifying persona. Capable of being the personification of charm one moment, his equal rage and almost limitless evil horrified even the most hardened of men the next. He was, in short, a tyrant of very capable means.

"*Who* are you and what are you doing in *my* city?" he asked, gesturing towards Giovanni and Otto.

With their arms raised, it was Giovanni who replied. "I am," he hesitated for the briefest of pauses, "Ferrante Uccello and this is my friend, Mauro."

With a gleam in his eye and a knowing and insincere smile that made no attempt to reach his eyes, Petrucci walked to within yards of the two men. "Liar!" he roared making the nearest crowd members still present flinch in fear. "If you are Ferrante Uccello, my friend, then you look very well for a ghost, and yet you expect me to believe that you are he? I wonder what we have here?" Placing his palms together in front of his face, his fingers touching his lips, he turned to his guards, "Take them!"

"And what of the actors' troupe, Sire?" asked the sergeant of the guard.

"Kill them. Kill them all for their treasonable behaviour," replied Petrucci mildly.

Certain braver and more foolhardy sectors of the crowd booed at the decision. "And kill anyone who defies my authority!" he thundered turning on the spot to face them. Suddenly afraid, the crowd's dissent turned into a barely audible murmur. In stunned silence the travelling performers were rounded up ready for execution, and Giovanni and Otto were removed for interrogation.

Scanning the rest of the crowd, Petrucci spied Isabella who was standing with her head bowed, desperately trying to conceal herself behind a stout, older man. Pointing at her he said quietly, "Bring her to me."

Siena, summer, 1483

Bound with chains and blindfolded, Giovanni and Otto were ushered through the darkened streets of Siena by elements of Petrucci's personal bodyguard, where they were led immediately to the city dungeons for interrogation.

"Forgive me Giovanni," said Otto hiccupping.

"Silence! There will be no talking between prisoners!" snarled the sergeant of the guard.

Before long the party had reached the forbidding building that housed the city dungeons. Marching through the main gate, both men were led down into a subterranean stygian world that was both stifling and oppressive. Shuffling slowly and hesitantly, Giovanni and Otto were taken deeper and deeper into the lower levels; their path led in every which way imaginable and before too long Giovanni had given up trying to remember the route.

Some quarter of an hour later, the small party stopped, and the blindfolds were roughly removed from both prisoners. Giovanni and Otto were pushed into a dank cell where there was barely sufficient headroom for them to stand. The only source of light was from a small lantern in the hallway outside. The door slammed shut behind them, and the key clicked in the lock, the noise reverberating in their ears. The two men listened as footsteps faded into the distance.

Still hiccupping, Otto sat down and sighed heavily. "Forgive me, my lord. We appear to be stuck. In vino veritas, I suppose," he said contritely.

"In vino veritas? Is that all you have to say for yourself?" muttered Giovanni fiercely. "The *truth*, as you like to put it, Otto, is that we now face death because you got roaring drunk, fell off the stage and revealed our presence to the world!"

Suitably chastised, Otto squatted on the stone floor, rubbing his sore head.

Giovanni was just able to make out the worried frown on his grizzled brow. "Anyway, what's the matter with you? You look like you've seen a ghost!" said Giovanni. "In fact, I've never seen you so perturbed. Nothing frightens you, Otto. Otto?"

Clearly distracted, the old mercenary blinked before a pained expression forced him to grit his teeth. "I've not seen that face for two decades, Giovanni." He paused. "Two decades of wondering. Two decades of hurt, anger and betrayal." He punched the cold stone wall of the cell, grazing his knuckles. "It was him, Giovanni. Petrucci's henchman is Konrad Haldur, my former commander, the butcher of Swabia himself. Even if he had not seen my face, he would have known my voice."

"Are you sure?" replied Giovanni, the concern discernible in his voice.

"I told you, I will never forget that face for as long as I live. Those murderous, predatory eyes of his... It makes sense now. It can only have been him, Giovanni. Haldur would've taken the greatest of pleasure in committing those murders. The sheer brutality of them... Haldur had a nickname in his native Hungary. They called him the 'Guta', a daemon of folklore native to those lands." Otto covered his face with his hands, and groaned. "What are we to do? These walls look impregnable. That door is three or four inches of solid oak at least."

Giovanni stood as tall as the low ceilinged cell would allow he walked over to the door and pressed his right ear against the cold wood, trying to listen for any movement outside. "Well, there's little use in worrying about him now. We're as good as dead if we can't escape from here, anyway," said Giovanni, his voice barely rising above a whisper. Sensing that his friend was still preoccupied, Giovanni turned his face from the door. "Shh!" he whispered. "I hear footsteps."

Before Giovanni had the chance to say more, the muffled footsteps halted outside the cell, and they heard indistinct voices. Their curiosity was answered as the cell door slowly creaked open and in walked their nemesis, the great tyrant himself.

"Come to gloat?" growled Otto, feeling decidedly less drunk and rather more hung over now.

With a feral sneer, Petrucci retorted, "Gloat? What an odd thing to say. I have no need for gloating. I hold the high ground here. If I were you, I would be less inclined to open my mouth and more inclined to wonder what was about to happen to me." Petrucci stood only feet away from where Otto squatted in front of him, looking him directly in the eye. "Now, you will tell me who you are and exactly why you are here, prying around in my city. I think we'll start with you, fat one," said the tyrant, pointing a finger at Otto.

Open-mouthed and with an offended look, Otto began to voice a retort, "I'm not fa—" but before he was able to finish his words, he was clubbed round the head and forced to his feet by two burly guards, both elite members of Petrucci's personal bodyguard who were in no mood for sparing the sensibilities of an old mercenary who had become a little too fond of his food and ale.

With his arms chained behind his back and flanked by the two guards, Otto was dragged from the cell and led away.

Giovanni stood up. "Where are you taking him?" he demanded, the shrillness of his voice hinting at panic.

With a sneer that revealed his true nature, Petrucci's eyes narrowed to slits. "Again, you are in no position to be demanding answers from me; rest assured, young man, it will be your turn soon enough." And with that, he bowed graciously, keeping his eyes fixed coldly on Giovanni before turning and leaving the cell. The cell door was slammed shut and Giovanni was left alone with his thoughts.

Slumping down onto what passed for a bed, Giovanni began to think about the events that had led to their capture and how, if at all possible, he could escape and rescue Otto. Plan after plan flitted through his mind, each as useless as the one before it. His thoughts, however, were interrupted by the sound of screaming. Sitting bolt upright, Giovanni shouted, "Otto!" before running to the door. Hammering away at it with his fists, he heard laughter from the other side. Peering through the small slit in the door, he made out Petrucci in the dim light sharing a joke with his guards, no doubt at poor Otto's expense. Lining his mouth up with the slit, Giovanni tried to spit at the mocking group but missed.

Finding even more amusement in this, Petrucci reiterated his promise to Giovanni. "Speak now, of your intentions here, and why you are in Siena, and I will end this and make your death as speedy and painless as possible." Pausing for effect and letting the words hang in the air, Petrucci continued, "Your friend will reveal all anyway, but you have the power to end his suffering and your own; I would suggest you cooperate. If you do *not*, I shall take it as a personal insult and ensure that you are tortured for days at a time. I will rain down hell itself upon you; your pain will be so great and so indescribable that death will seem like a welcome relief."

With a grimace and a snarl of anger and frustration, Petrucci turned on his heel and stalked off without saying another word.

Giovanni sank back down onto his bed in despair.

An hour later Otto was dragged back to his cell and dumped unceremoniously onto the cold stone floor. Rushing to his friend's side, Giovanni hauled the older man onto the bed to allow him to rest. "What did they do to you?" asked Giovanni.

"Nothing I could not handle," Otto smiled weakly, revealing a mouth that was badly bloodied. "They knew we were coming. It seems that their spy was most efficient in identifying us, even before we had left Florence. They do not know why we are here, though.

They have their suspicions, however. That, I fear, is the information they will want from you."

Giovanni replied, "Otto, we must not reveal why we are here. If they are aware that Florence knows something is afoot, they will no doubt accelerate their plans before we have sufficient time to respond."

Breathing heavily and clearly in pain, Otto's bloody smile told of a thousand unspoken words. "Then we need to ensure that doesn't happen," he said.

Nodding his head in agreement, Giovanni said, "I have the feeling we'll be finding out soon enough, old friend."

Siena, summer, 1483

The inner sanctum of the Tyrant of Siena was lavish luxury indeed. The air was heavy with the scent of the finest incenses and perfumes. Marble floors dotted with sumptuous woven silk rugs lent a stately air to the chambers, while the finest paintings from some of the most renowned artists adorned the walls. Vast, airy rooms filled with furniture carved from exotic woods found only in the Southern Indies and the ceiling was supported by huge marble pillars signifying great wealth and strength.

It was in one of these rooms that a captive Isabella reclined on a long sofa covered in the finest of velvets. On a nearby table lay sumptuous foods and the very finest in local Tuscan wine. It was clear that Petrucci had become attracted to the young spy even though he clearly didn't trust her. She was chained to the floor and had a two-man guard placed upon her.

After some time of waiting, Isabella's concentration started to wander. She was abruptly reminded of her situation when Petrucci's entourage entered unannounced, preceding the man himself.

"Ah, my dear girl, I trust you have been looked after? Forgive my lateness, but I have been taking care of some business," he said speaking eloquently – ever the charming, debonair gentleman when it suited him. Perceiving the look of fear on the young woman's face he continued, "It simply won't do to keep company such as that, you know. A beautiful young lady could get hurt if she fell in with the wrong crowd." Letting his words sink in, he continued, "If you were to reveal to me the nature of your association with them, I could protect you from any un-pleasantries that may arise from this situation."

Finding her voice and courage at last, Isabella replied, "I barely know them my lord. I only met them just before the performance began. You must believe me, surely?" She cringed inside as she realised how desperate her words sounded. At the same time a peculiar distant look crossed the face of the great tyrant.

"I believe you, my dear," said Petrucci consolingly. "I believe that you are somehow, in some way, in league with those two men in my dungeons, and if I have to cut off your pretty head to persuade them to talk, I shall do so. Now, does that change things?"

Isabella rediscovered her strength and her anger flared. "How dare you threaten me, you bastard!" she hissed.

Smirking, Petrucci replied, "Oh, I'm not threatening you. I'm *promising* you that this will happen if you don't tell me who you are, and why you are here. Perhaps I ought to reveal to you my intentions to provoke you into talking. Would that help?" Isabella looked away, unwilling to meet the piercing gaze of the mad tyrant in front of her. With an all too familiar feral grin, Petrucci merely replied, "Take her away!" and the young Venetian was unchained and then whisked off her feet and dragged kicking and screaming down to the dungeons where Giovanni and Otto were imprisoned.

Republic of Florence, summer, 1483

Two days' ride to the north, in Florence, a panicked meeting of the Signoria was in session. The nine men and their aides and advisors sat round a large table in the heart of the Palazzo Vecchio. Shouts and cries of despair were heard throughout the debating chamber for news of Giovanni's and Otto's capture as well as that of Isabella's had been received.

"We must mobilise the army. I have heard enough to know that whatever threat Siena presents, if indeed it is Siena, must be imminent!" cried one man.

"Attack Siena!" cried another.

In the centre of the room, one man stood up from his seated position. Piero Bartolo De Larosa, the Gonfaloniere of Justice called for order, raised his arms and summoned all of his gravitas to quieten the room. "Friends, colleagues, we must remain on alert, for whatever evil is building in that city is surely upon us; but we cannot, must not, jump at shadows. It would be prudent for us to issue an alert to our army and to mobilise it, but it would also be prudent that we do so as quietly as possible so that we do not betray our hand."

This brought an instant response from Salvatore Lombardi, the head of the Arte Del Cambio. "A pre-emptive strike on Siena now would remove any threat to Florence. We cannot afford to waste time here when the day of action is upon us!"

For several long hours the debate raged while the fear and anger in the room were palpable. The general consensus was that to take no action was not an option;

equally however, Florence found herself caught in a trap. If she mobilised her armies and laid siege to Sienna, her rear was vulnerable to attack from the likes of Pisa.

The city itself seemed paralysed by fear and indecision. Traders shut their stores earlier than normal and the citizens of Florence were afraid to walk the streets after dark lest their fate be that of the merchants who had been murdered in such a brutal manner. Mothers protectively ushered their children from one place to the next without lingering or stopping to talk to friends. Tensions ran high when fights broke out in the streets, and people suspected their friends or neighbours of being spies or assassins. Whilst the Signoria debated into the small hours, their forces struggled to retain control of the city as the atmosphere reached near-riotous fever pitch.

After much deliberation and many very heated arguments, the Signoria decided against a full-scale invasion and siege of Siena and opted instead to have the city's army of condottiere patrol the streets to instil a sense of order and calm after the previous day's troubles, whilst remaining on full alert to any potential developments. It was, with ever increasing anxiety, that the Signoria awaited any developments from Siena.

Siena, summer, 1483

The door slammed hard against the wall, waking both Giovanni and Otto from their deep slumber with a start. Isabella was flung into the small room, landing heavily on the stone floor. Both men got to their feet somewhat groggily and went over to the prone woman checking that she was unhurt.

Beyond the door stood Petrucci wearing his full state regalia. Stooping down and entering the cell, surrounded by his guards, the cell that was cramped before became even more so.

"Dear friends, I feel that we may have started off on the wrong foot. Let us begin again in the spirit of co-operation," he said with a broad smile on his face. "Allow me to start by saying that I may not have been telling you the entire truth. You, specifically," he said pointing at Giovanni. "My agents in Florence inform me that you were seen entering and leaving the Palazzo Vecchio and that you were also seen entering what we believe is the Palazzo Lascorza. If this is true, then I think a logical deduction to make here is that you are Lascorza the younger and that this," he said pointing to Otto, "is your aide and former condottiero of Florence, Otto Baldwinson. Am I right, Giovanni?" Before Giovanni could reply, Petrucci continued, "However, this young lady still presents a mystery to me, and that vexes me greatly. What is *her* role here?" he paused momentarily. "I would advise that you tell me the truth or you will find my patience runs thin, and her life will be forfeit, here and now."

Giovanni turned and looked at Otto who shook his head as a warning, although the motion was barely discernible. Turning back to Petrucci, Giovanni replied, "I do not know this Giovanni Lascorza of whom you speak."

"Enough!" roared Petrucci. "You have insulted my intelligence for long enough, I think." Nodding to the guards he ordered, "Take her, do what you will with her, and display her head on the battlements when you have finished with her."

Leaping to his feet, Giovanni pleaded for her life, his arms held out in supplication. "Enough! Enough… please, I beg of you. I will tell you everything that I know, but you must promise to spare her. I have no knowledge of her truly; we met before the performance in the Piazza Del Campo. That is the truth of the matter. My name *is* indeed Giovanni Lascorza; I am the son of the late former Gonfaloniere of Florence, Alessandro Lascorza. I was hired by the Signoria of Florence to spy on the inhabitants of Siena for commercial and reasons of trade and import. And you were correct again; this is my aide and friend Otto Baldwinson."

Petrucci stood, rubbing his chin, a range of emotions flitting across his face. "Hmm, partially true at least, I suspect. I do not see why Florence would go to such lengths for a mere trade dispute. I think there is more to it than that. I think you're here to investigate the murders of those merchants in Florence. Such a crying shame that these circumstances should arise, don't you think?"

The blood drained from Giovanni's face as he realised that Petrucci had all along known far more than he had let on and had merely been playing with them for his own sick, personal pleasure.

"There is much that I know, young Lascorza, especially as it was *I* who ordered those very same murders for a very good reason, as I'm sure you'll agree. It was necessary, but regrettable, that I had to include your father, too." Petrucci waited for the meaning of his words to make sense to Giovanni.

His face revealing first horror and then sheer, blinding rage, Giovanni lashed out like a coiled snake directly at Petrucci's face. His father had been murdered, the man standing before him had actually *ordered* his father's death! "Bastard!" he screamed. The guards fought to restrain Giovanni as he thrashed around hurling invectives and vitriol at Petrucci, all the while desperately trying to reach him.

Laughing uncontrollably, the tyrant signalled for Giovanni to be stopped. Instantly obeying the command, one of the guards slammed a gauntleted fist into Giovanni's abdomen. Writhing in pain, Giovanni fell to the floor, dry heaving and fighting for breath.

"Now that you have calmed down, perhaps we might talk as civilised men? For many years now, I have watched as the fortunes of Florence swelled and my own fair city's waned. I have watched the endless territorial expansion of your city and, for many years, I have seen your merchants stroll around *my* city as though they owned it. I have watched this uneasy peace between our two cities bring Florence nothing but prosperity and my city nothing but ruin. I have watched with bitterness as the greatness I predicted for my city was stolen by yours. The finest artists, thinkers, architects, poets and politicians of our time all flocked to Florence to find their fame and fortune whilst Siena was seen as little more than a backwater."

Petrucci had begun to pace around the entrance to the tiny cell. Giovanni was still on his knees, his long hair now lank and hanging down over his face, and breathing raggedly, raged silently.

"Of course, I could not allow this outrage to continue," Petrucci persisted, "so I hatched a plan that would remove the hegemony that controlled your city, your vaunted, supposedly democratic republic, for ever. I even used your own merchants against you, then had them eliminated. I employed the finest merchants from Florence to seek out very special cargoes in the distant lands of the Orient, cargoes so valuable to me that I paid a high premium for them, a very high premium indeed."

Giovanni's curiosity gained the better of him, and for a moment of icy calm, he listened closely to the story that Petrucci told.

The tyrant continued his tale. "I have arranged for an entire fleet of ships from the Orient to sail towards the River Arno where the cargo, the precious cargo, will be safely delivered to Florence, a most precious and deadly cargo."

It was Otto's turn to be incredulous. "What are you driving at, you mad man? What precious and deadly cargo? What have you done?"

"As old as you are, I doubt even you would recall the Black Death personally, Otto Baldwinson, but I'm sure it is indelibly engraved into the psyche of the people of Florence, and for much of the rest of Europe, in fact. To cut to the heart of the matter, I have dozens, maybe hundreds of plague-infested bodies within the holds of my fleet heading towards Florence as we speak. The ships are disguised as simple merchant ships so as not to arouse any suspicion. They will sail down the Arno and straight into the heart of Florence itself, whereby the cargo will be unloaded and the contagion left to do its work. The disease will spread, quite literally like the plague, through the streets and piazzas of your city. Your people will drop like flies, laid waste by the Black Death itself. Once that aim has been achieved, my armies will be placed on standby so that when the great city of Florence lies broken and dying, we will lay siege to it and burn it to the ground, thus erasing and obliterating Florence from the history books in a matter of days."

Petrucci paused.

"I consider this to be a rather fitting end to a city that has been a thorn in the side of my city for longer than I care to remember. I am led to believe that this will be a most agreeable set of circumstances to Cesare Borgia also; he has long sought some form of solution to the Florentine problem, and I rather hope to curry favour with him. Giovanni there is more that you must hear…"

Stopping now for breath, Petrucci flashed a toothy, malevolent grin before resuming. "Your father was a man much respected in Florence. His word carried significant weight even though he was no longer a member of the Signoria itself. He was also one of the few men in Florence who could potentially have pieced together my plans and so, in order for them to come to fruition, I could not allow him to live... As for the merchants, they simply knew too much; you understand, I'm sure. As for your father it was nothing personal, just business."

Open-mouthed and still gasping a little for air and saliva, Giovanni could barely bring himself to speak "You... you murdered my father for the sake of business. My father, those merchants; you would murder all of Florence, for what, your city and your pride? You are insane, and I will stop you. I *will* find a way to stop you. The people in this city are terrified of you and your regime. They despise your rule; if I fail, *they* will find a way to stop you!" he spat.

"That's as may be, young man, but very soon, you and your friends here will be dead and your city will be wiped from the map, and there is nothing that you or any other earthly being can do to prevent this. When I have removed Florence as a threat, I shall rule this entire region without peer. Absolute power will be *mine*. Not even the Papal States or the Milanese would dare intervene against me!" Petrucci laughed.

Mediterranean Sea, summer, 1483

In the deep, dark blue Mediterranean Sea, a fleet of galleys headed for the pristine beaches and emerald green and brown fields of the Tuscan coast. The waves crashed against the bulk of the merchant ships as their deadly, stinking cargo lay putrefying in their holds. In the distance, lay the mouth to the River Arno, signalling the fleet's final route towards Florence.

The captain of the fleet, Hai Jiang, was a short weather-worn man from the Orient who, by the apparent ease with which he maintained his balance in the rough seas, was a seasoned and worldly sailor. Privately though, even he questioned whether he had the stomach for his current task.

His first mate turned to him whilst watching over the bow of the ship. "We must make the coast by nightfall, the fewer people that see us, the better."

Nodding his agreement, the captain spoke. "Yes, I do not think it wise that we should let down this Petrucci. He *scares* me more than any man I've ever met. Nor do I trust him; let's deliver this cargo and then our part of this bargain is done and we can be on our way. It's dangerous to make a pact with the devil."

The first mate shivered, and it was not due to the biting sea breeze.

Looking out over the dozen ships in his fleet, the captain gave the order to signal the approach to the mouth of the river. The ships of the fleet moved into the best approximation of line astern as merchantmen could before sailing into the mouth of the Arno.

Siena, summer, 1484

The streets of Siena were becoming increasingly crowded; the news of the impending execution of the spies from Florence had spread like wildfire. The crowds cheered and jeered as performers and orators that had been hired for just that purpose whipped the crowd up into a veritable frenzy.

In the city's dungeons, Giovanni, Otto and Isabella were being readied for their execution. Their bonds were checked, hessian bags placed over their heads, and a heavy guard was placed upon them as they were taken to the Piazza Del Campo in the very heart of Siena.

Otto had accepted the last rites, although Giovanni as a defiant gesture and exile from the seminary had declined. Isabella had not said anything to anyone, seemingly still in denial and shock over her impending death. They were led into an open courtyard where they joined other prisoners. Accompanied by a guard, each prisoner climbed awkwardly into one of the carts used to transport them to the centre of the city.

Passing through the gates of the prisons and into the streets, the crowd reacted instantly, throwing rotten fruit and dung at the prisoners, booing and jeering and hurling insults all the while. The cacophony of noise grew to a crescendo and was as deafening as the heat was oppressive. There was no breeze; no fresh gusts of air that sometimes made summer in Tuscany bearable. The Piazza Del Campo continued to fill up with people, and wild animals chained to posts set in the hard cobbled ground roared their defiance, adding to the grim spectacle of death.

Many hundreds of soldiers lined the route to the Piazza Del Campo, keeping the crowds in check. Even so, progress was initially slow, but, eventually, the procession of carts and prisoners made good speed to the centre of the city, where the great tyrant himself was waiting with his entourage and personal bodyguard.

The carts finally reached the execution ground where the condemned, hands still tightly bound, were unloaded and then led in single file up onto the raised wooden scaffolds.

It had been decreed that the prisoners were to be decapitated. The executioner performing the grizzly task was a non-descript man with a brown leather mask covering all of his face, save his eyes. Some of the prisoners wailed and moaned, begging and pleading for forgiveness and release. Others remained stoic in the face of their own death. The executioner slowly and methodically ground his axe against the grindstone, ensuring that his blade was fully sharpened and ignored all the pleas. He was but one of several executioners earning their pay that day.

Petrucci had taken centre stage and, with his arms raised, he gestured for the crowd to be still so that he might address them. The hubbub died away and silence reigned. "Friends, colleagues, fellow citizens of Siena, we gather today to right a wrong that our great, old enemy, Florence has perpetrated against us. We have learned that some of these prisoners you see lined up before you today were sent by that accursed city to spy on us, to report back to Florence our every move. Others here were paid by Florence to spread dissent and to disrupt our day-to-day lives as best they could. They did this out of hate for us and out of sheer malice. Florence will not stop until it sees us destroyed, and for that reason, we must defend ourselves!"

By now the fervour of the crowd had been whipped into a frenzy of emotion, with people baying for blood, desperate for vengeance against an imaginary, non-existent foe. Pointing to Giovanni, Otto and Isabella the tyrant continued. "These three in particular are worthy of your hatred; as agents of Florence, they sought to overthrow my rule, and for that, they deserve our utmost contempt. Let justice commence!"

With these words the slow, hypnotic, repetitive beat of drums started up in readiness for the grisly retribution.

Petrucci raised his hand and dropped it again in one fluid motion. Further down the line from Giovanni and his companions, the killing commenced. A further dozen executioners with swords and axes raised their weapons high above their heads and bought them down with such incredible force the wood beneath some prisoner's necks splintered also. Some in the crowd roared their approval as arterial blood gushed and sprayed over the first few rows, whilst some of the crowd, notably the relatives of the executed, wailed and cried in despair.

A man with a gruff voice grabbed Giovanni none too gently by the shoulders and forced him to his knees in front of a block. In a calm voice, he uttered the words, "This will take but a moment."

With the sacking, covering his head, removed, Giovanni closed his eyes and placing his head on the rough wooden chopping block, he turned it to the side as instructed, awaiting the blade. His heart thudded violently in his chest as he tried desperately to swallow; never in all his life had he been so afraid and he tried and failed desperately to reach for any semblance of faith that had sustained him in his tender years. Drums from the city guard played in the background. Moments passed as hours and time slowed. Every beat of Giovanni's heart thudded and echoed in his ears.

Managing to make out faces in the crowd, Giovanni deliberated briefly upon death, how it would feel, and considered the circumstances that had led him to that moment. Casting his eyes over towards Otto, he saw that the large man was struggling, desperately trying to reach him. The sun slipped from behind a cloud and shone fiercely in Giovanni's eyes, blinding him. The executioner stood over Lascorza the younger, raised the mighty blade and with a grunt of effort, swung the blade high over his head and brought it crashing through the shoulder of the nearest guard.

Pulling the mask from his face the executioner revealed a proud, handsome face with aquiline features. At his signal, armed men leapt from the crowd and stage hacking at the guards around them, bringing death and destruction to all who stood against them.

Grabbing hold of Giovanni, Giacomo dragged him to his feet and loosened his bonds. "Signor Lascorza, it is an honour to meet you. I have little time to explain, but you and your associates must leave this place at once for Siena is now at war with itself. My men and I will attempt to hold Petrucci back, but I cannot guarantee for how long."

Pandolfo Petrucci stood up from the purple plush velvet-covered seat as the action on the gibbet unfolded. His face distorted into something akin to that of a snarling feral beast. "What is happening?" he roared. "Stop them! Kill them all!"

Soldiers and city guards hurried in every direction frantically giving orders and drawing weapons, searching wildly for an unidentifiable enemy. The crowd in the Piazza Del Campo began to panic and scream in fright, caught in what had become a frenzy of violence as Giacomo's men fought the city guards in the employ of Petrucci. The sound of blade on blade rang out over the square and the screams of the dying, wounded and terrified were piteous to hear.

Amongst this melee, Giovanni, Otto and Isabella frantically tried to make good their escape. Fighting their way through the crowds and guards, Giovanni yelled across to Giacomo, "Petrucci revealed his ultimate plan to us. He intends to destroy Florence and become overlord of this entire region. He seeks to curry favour with the Borgia also. We *must* not allow this to happen."

Shaking his head, whilst parrying a sword blow aimed at his neck, Giacomo answered breathlessly, "Then it is imperative you warn the authorities in Florence of his intentions, my friend. You can do no more here. This fight is ours alone."

With a savage sweep of his newly acquired blade, Giovanni cut down his nearest opponent. He glanced over at Otto only to see him in the thick of the fight, back-to-back with Isabella who was, it seemed, equally as capable with a blade as Otto. Her slender, yet deadly fast and accurate form whipped and lashed out her sword with consummate finesse; whereas Otto's immense strength saw him cut a swathe through the ranks of Petrucci's guards like a scythe through a row of corn.

Sprinting through the streets of Siena, the intrepid group, desperate to elude Petrucci, ran as fast as the conditions enabled them to. Meanwhile, the guards began hauling the huge gates shut as quickly as possible. Spying two unattended horses, Otto grabbed the reins and almost threw Isabella up onto the back of the nearest, whilst holding the other horse for Giovanni. "We have to leave now, Signor!" cried Otto, looking decidedly more aggravated than Giovanni had seen him in a long while.

Giovanni took Giacomo by the shoulders and said, "Come with us friend. You can oppose Petrucci from Florence. Help us to help you defeat him!"

"My place is here, amongst my people, Giovanni. I thank you for your offer, but I cannot leave them now in this hour. Besides, I owe Petrucci an agonising and painful death; perhaps I will explain one day if we live through this one and the next."

Embracing briefly, both men made their hurried farewells.

Leaping up onto the back of his horse, Giovanni kicked it into a gallop, quickly catching up with Otto and Isabella who were careering towards the gates that loomed in front of them.

A large contingent of guards armed with long spears had assembled in front of the north gate forming a loose phalanx. No sooner had they assembled than a hail of arrows flew through the air towards them. Giacomo had deployed his men wisely and had concealed some in side streets, buildings and alleyways facing onto the gate, and it was these who now cut down many of the guards.

Making the most of the diversion, both horses were spurred on through the closing gap between the gates. Their riders leaned low in the saddles and rode hard in the direction of Florence. Arrows flew past the riders, some missing them by so little that they heard their whine and felt the slight disturbance of air as they whizzed past.

River Arno, summer, 1483

Inching closer to its destination, the merchant fleet sailed slowly through the murky waters of the River Arno. In the holds, the deadly cargo had begun to stink and this had not gone unnoticed by the crews of the vessels.

"Captain Jiang, this is getting out of hand. I understand that we are mere hours away from our destination, but this is almost beyond the men's ability to withstand," said Hai Jiang's executive officer.

"You may inform the men that when we are finished here, they will each of them be rich beyond reckoning. Then they may do whatever they please, with whomever they please, however they please. I only demand that they maintain full concentration until the task at hand is complete."

Looking pensive Jiang continued, "And with that in mind, please ensure that all preparations to transport the cargo ashore have been made. Things may become complicated, and I wish to be prepared for any eventuality."

Nodding, the executive officer replied, "Sir..." and hurried to relay his orders. Looking out over the banks, not for the first time, Jiang wished that this particular assignment was over.

Several hours passed and there, looming into sight on the horizon, lay the bejewelled city of Florence itself. Her walls stood like a beacon, a bastion of democratic hope surrounded by barbarous neighbours. Her citizens knew relative freedom and peace, freedom to choose their own path in life, freedom to elect their own officials.

Turning to his executive officer who stood at a respectful distance, Captain Jiang spoke, a smug grin on his face. "I almost regret doing this old friend; I hear Florence is unrivalled in her way of life, her artists and architects, thinkers and politicians, but when I think of the *money* we are promised, I have no further qualms about our course of action. It is, just business."

Agreeing, the first mate replied, "It is indeed sir, just business. Besides, you can look back on this and see it as a defining moment in your life. How many can truly say they have been present at the death of a city, especially a magnificent pearl like Florence? One day, men will speak of this moment, and your name shall be uttered alongside the names of the men who engineered this entire episode."

With a derisory snort, the captain replied, "I'm not so sure that is an accolade I care for, old friend. Let us complete the deed before we sing our own praises; are the men ready, have full preparations been made to unload the cargo as quickly as possible?"

The response was a curt nod and a simple, "The fleet and men are ready. Full preparations have been made."

"Good. Then stand by to come alongside within the hour. It would appear," said Jiang pointing to the horizon, "that our destiny draws near."

The wilds of Tuscany, summer, 1483

Riding like the wind, Giovanni, Otto and Isabella did not spare their horses the whip. They could not, for riding in pursuit were men of the mercenary cavalry employed by Siena, forty men in total, heavily armed although lightly armoured. They were, in effect, scouts; not as quick as their targets, but able to maintain contact with them none the less, simply by following the trail their horses left. Behind them, the larger body of cavalry, some several hundred strong, rode. Finally, roughly an hour's march behind and bringing up the rear, marched over four thousand Sienese mercenaries. The heavy tread of their marching footsteps echoed around the surrounding plains.

At the head of his cavalry was the arch tyrant himself, Pandolfo Petrucci. Clad in his finest, most ornate plate armour, and carrying a lance in his right hand, he watched his standard bearer carry his personal coat of arms, the banner fluttering in the warm summer breeze.

The tyrant's plans had been thrown into disarray with the arrival of the young Florentine and his Germanic aide, and Petrucci had fully resolved to make them and the city of Florence pay in kind. Riding back towards the main bulk of his army, he called out to his troops. "Onwards, onwards to fortune and glory, show no mercy you murdering bastards. Show no mercy, and take your place in history!"

A huge roar greeted him, and the dust that was kicked up from their feet was visible as a haze for miles around.

Several miles ahead, Giovanni, Otto and Isabella struggled to stay ahead of the following Sienese scouts. Giovanni leaned over and shouted, "We have to lose them. We'll never make Florence at this rate! There are far too many for us to fight off!" Spying a ravine in the distance, Giovanni directed his horse in its direction and spurred it on even more. "Over there, we can try and lose them in that!" he yelled.

Following Giovanni, Otto spurred his horse in the same direction and made for the ravine as fast as his horse could manage considering that it was carrying two people.

Having made the temporary safety of the ravine, the trio dismounted from their steeds and hid amongst the thick bushes and scrub. Watching the Sienese scouts pass by from behind the safety of a thick gorse bush, Isabella whispered, "They've gone; we should be able to lay low for a while and take a different route."

"We don't have time for that," replied Otto. "Before we know it, they'll realise we've doubled back, and they'll do the same. It's a standard procedure if they suspect they've been flanked." As Otto's military knowledge was unsurpassed, his word in this matter stood unchallenged.

Nodding his agreement, Giovanni pointed at the stragglers in the scouting party. "What about those, they look promising?" he said.

With a feral grin, Otto slapped the younger man on the arm and cried, "That's my boy. Now you're thinking!"

Looking confused, Isabella retorted, "What looks promising? What *are* you both talking about? What looks promising?" A look of horror spread over Isabella's face. "Oh no, no, no, no, that's insane!" she blurted. "Are you in all seriousness suggesting that we attack the rear of this column and somehow assume their position within the ranks? Then what? We sneak up to the very walls of Florence where archers will, no doubt, be on the lookout for men dressed such as these before being shot by our own side? And in case you hadn't noticed, I'm a woman!"

A wry smile by Giovanni and Otto was all the reply needed.

Republic of Florence, summer, 1483

The centre of Florence was a hive of activity. Troops took up defensive positions; supplies were taken to the city walls and gates, full preparations for siege warfare were being made. Nothing was left to chance and Gonfaloniere De Larosa himself personally oversaw the work. He stood with the Priori of the Arte Del Cambio, Salvatore Lombardi in the Piazza Della Signoria. "Is there any word of Lascorza and his aide?" said De Larosa.

"Nothing, no sign of him as yet; we lost contact with them a few days ago. The last reports that we have state that they were captured by Petrucci's men before being imprisoned and were due to be executed shortly. I fear it might be too late for them, old friend. We must look to our own resources and the city's defences now. How do they proceed?" asked Lombardi.

"As well as can be expected for such short notice Signor; however, it grieves me to think that the city has lost such fine servants as the young Lascorza and his old aide. I knew the lad's father well. This is no fitting end for him, and I can say that most assuredly." De Larosa paused before voicing his next words. "We must also be prepared for the fact that we may lose the day here; we still have little idea as to the exact nature of the forces that we're facing. I have mobilised the city guard, halved rations at the gates and walls in preparation for a siege situation, and called in more grain and fresh water also. The citizens that live outside the walls have also been given the option to come within the walls or escape the area. I wished to avoid panic and fear on the streets of Florence, but I suspect I am a month or so too late for that," the Gonfaloniere continued with a weak smile.

Both men walked towards the Palazzo Vecchio. Salvatore Lombardi spoke as they walked. "We must inform the rest of the Signoria of this development. How many others know of Lascorza's execution?"

"None, you and I are the only ones who have been notified. The remaining Signoria are only aware that they had been captured. It will come as a blow indeed. The *last* thing this city needs is news of this nature."

As they approached the entrance to the Palazzo Vecchio the guards snapped to attention before ushering both men inside. Walking through the long marble corridors into the main assembly hall, the two men came to a halt in front of the gathered congress.

The murmuring from the crowd ceased when De Larosa and Lombardi entered the room. "Friends, brothers," said De Larosa quietly, "I'm afraid we have some ill-timed news. It has been brought to our attention that the young Lascorza and his aide have been captured by Petrucci's forces and have either been executed or are about to be at any time. There can be no question that the plan to reveal the true nature of events here has been seriously hampered. The remainder of our spy network in Siena has revealed little else to us; it was our fervent hope that by sending Signor's Lascorza and Baldwinson, we would get to the very heart of this deceit once and for all. Now it seems, we are blind and deaf, but not without hope. Our militia forces are at full readiness for war, supplies and rations are in plentiful supply, and our allies have been made aware in advance of our circumstances and stand ready to come to our aid. All is not lost."

Rising from his seat, a man in the crowd spoke. "Signor De Larosa, you tell us that all is well and that we are prepared for any eventuality, but we lack any credible intelligence. What if we mobilise our army and nothing happens, what of the costs? What happens if this is nothing but a trade dispute between rival merchants' guilds and we were to invade and lay siege to Siena as a pre-emptive strike? What then? We stand on the verge of war and have no idea of exactly who, what and why we're fighting, I mean no disrespect, Gonfaloniere, but I would say that we are far from well. In fact, I would say that we are fighting blind and that we would do well to pray for salvation and strength to face whatever daemons lurk in the darkness."

A murmur of agreement rippled round the great meeting hall of the Palazzo Vecchio. Several jeers could also be heard as some of the guild members made their disapproval of the situation known.

Gonfaloniere De Larosa struck his staff on the tiled floor, the echo carrying round the vast space. "That is enough! We cannot and must not jump at shadows, I agree. We must equally, however, stand ready for any threat that may materialise. By maintaining a watchful vigil, we will not be caught unawares. Nor shall we overreact. A precise and measured response is what the situation demands, and a precise and measured response is what is being deployed as we speak. There is little more that can be done in terms of preparation I assure you."

A roar of dissent reverberated around the meeting chamber in response to De Larosa's words when a messenger hurried in and presented himself before the Gonfaloniere himself.

"Sir Gonfaloniere, I have an urgent message from our spies in Siena."

De Larosa nodded a curt thanks to the messenger before eyeing the scroll in his hand with a mixture of caution and fear. De Larosa snatched the message, hurriedly ripped open the wax seal and began to read the words inside. A sharp intake of breath indicated that the news was not good, or at the very least, was less than ideal.

The Gonfaloniere of Justice, scroll in hand, sat down, with a crestfallen look on his face and called for calm from the chamber. "It seems that events have forced our hand. The army of Siena has mobilised and is marching on Florence as we speak; the numbers according to our best intelligence appear to be in the order of several hundred cavalry, and anything between seven to ten thousand infantrymen. Of Lascorza and Baldwinson there is no further news, war is upon us."

The momentary stunned, hushed silence in the meeting chamber was broken by yet another cacophony of shouting and arguing.

With his face in his hands, De Larosa realised that now more than ever, decisive leadership had to be shown. He rose to his feet and called his advisors and supporters to him and convened a full council of war.

The wilds of Tuscany, summer, 1483

From the protective cover of the ravine, Giovanni, Otto and Isabella singled out their targets. A small group of stragglers had become separated from the main scouting force and had let their defences drop. Letting out a shrill whistle, Otto climbed out of the gorge and openly beckoned to the cavalrymen in front of him. "Hey there, yes you, you useless sacks of skin. Over here!" Otto cried.

Needing little further invite, the cavalrymen bore down on him, covering the rough chalky ground in seconds, their lances aimed squarely at the squat Germanic mercenary. With no warning, the closest rider to Otto fell back from his saddle as a fist sized rock hit him squarely in the face. Armoured or not, the man was clearly stunned as he landed heavily on the ground.

Rushing from her hiding place behind a nearby tree, Isabella stood over the prone cavalryman and thrust her lethally sharp blade through his chest with all her might, piercing his ornate armour. Sitting almost bolt upright and clutching his chest, the cavalryman screamed in agony once before slumping to the ground, dead. Pulling the blade from his body, Isabella rolled out of the way as another of the horsemen thrust his lance towards her own chest. Deflecting the lance, Isabella struck the horse's front legs with her blade as it shot past her. Whinnying in pain, the horse fell forward throwing its rider several feet through the air and onto the ground with such force that his neck broke upon impact. Seeing the lifeless body, Isabella turned to see Giovanni and Otto fighting back-to-back against the remaining three scouts who had dismounted. Fending off a high blow aimed at his skull, Giovanni slid his blade skilfully away before bringing it back and sliding it across the stomach of the unfortunate cavalryman, instantly disembowelling him.

Otto shouted across at the younger man, "Try not to ruin the uniforms too much; we need to be convincing should we encounter others!"

With a shrug, Giovanni kicked another cavalryman between the legs before backhanding him across the face with the pommel of his sword. "Is that better?" he replied with a grin.

The sole remaining cavalryman surrendered his blade and dropped to his knees, pleading for mercy. Otto, taking an unusually lenient view of the matter, knocked the cowering man out with a single, nose breaking punch, before tying and gagging him and hiding him out of sight in the ravine.

"There, that takes care of that," said Otto with a beaming grin, rubbing his hands together.

"I wouldn't be so sure, old friend," replied Giovanni, clearing his throat apologetically and pointing at the assembled uniforms that had been stripped from the cooling bodies. "It may prove difficult to find one that fits you."

Otto threw him a withering look as he struggled into a surcoat from the largest of the slain cavalrymen.

Isabella showed no such hesitation in removing her clothing, revealing a dark-skinned complexion and soft, delicate body that clearly belied its lethal potential.

Catching a sideways glance from Giovanni, there was a clear, palpable tension in the air as the glance lingered.

Realising somewhat belatedly that he was now staring at her, Giovanni hurriedly finished putting on his uniform, wiping away as much of the gore from it as he could. Otto had, with not a little cursing and grunting squeezed himself into his doublet and looked less than entirely pleased about the situation.

The bodies of the slain men were hidden out of sight behind rocks and covered with branches and scrub; the drag marks made by their feet were expunged.

Then, stifling a smirk at Otto's expense, Giovanni spoke, "We must ride hard for Florence. When we encounter the main scouting force, make no eye contact or sudden movements, try to remain as calm as is humanly possible. They will still be on the lookout for us dressed as we were; if we can get past them, we can make direct progress towards Florence and put an end to this once and for all."

Mounting his newly acquired chestnut-coloured horse, Otto remarked casually, "And if they spot us?"

Nodding in agreement, Isabella called out to Giovanni who was manoeuvring his horse carefully through the thick bramble bushes and onto the nearby chalky track. "Yes, what if they spot us still?"

Pausing for a moment whilst turning his head to one side, Giovanni replied with a low voice, "Then we're each of us on our own. You must make your way to Florence as best you can."

Republic of Florence, summer, 1483

Gonfaloniere De Larosa sat at the end of a long table in the Palazzo Vecchio, his counsel of war called, his advisors present, the room abuzz with heated discussion and disagreement.

One of De Larosa's senior advisors was a former Swiss condottiero by the name of Marti Urs. Tall, imposing and powerfully built, his knowledge of the military arts was almost unrivalled. Rising to his feet, he spoke with confidence. "We should meet them on the field, Signor Gonfaloniere, and spare Florence a protracted siege that will serve no-one. By meeting them and defeating them decisively thus, we spare our citizens the suffering and deprivation that a siege would bring if we were to hide behind our walls. With your consent Gonfaloniere, I should like to volunteer to lead our forces against Siena."

A brief murmur of consent arose from the room, yet a dissenting voice raised itself above the murmur. "And what if our army should lose the day? What if it is, to all intents and purposes, destroyed? We risk leaving the entire city defenceless; we talk of sparing the citizens of this city any hardships, yet I can see things being much harder for them should the army be wiped out. Who would defend us then?"

A hushed silence descended; all faces turned to the man at the end of the room. Clearing his throat, De Larosa stayed the hand of his Swiss condottiere. "Please, forgive my ignorance Signor, but you are?"

The dissenting voice belonged to a man in his early to mid-twenties, handsome in appearance, and clad in robes of the finest crimson silk. "I am Fabio Moretto; I have recently joined your staff, Signor Gonfaloniere. Forgive me if I was speaking out of turn, but if meeting the armies of Siena on the field were to lead to our defeat, Florence would be doomed; our streets would run red with blood, and the slaughter of innocents at the hands of our enemies would be great."

"So what would you have me do? It's all very well to disagree, but I require answers, not dissent," replied De Larosa.

Glancing around the room, Fabio Moretto's eyes darted from one face to the next, looking for an ally, anyone who would agree with his suggestions. Yet he found none. Any and all eye contact was broken the moment it met. With a resigned shrug of his shoulders, Moretto continued. "We bar the gates, line the walls with archers, and keep the main bulk of our army ready to respond to any breaches that might occur. Let the Sienese crash against our walls and let them blunt their attack upon them."

Slamming his fist upon the heavy oak table, Urs spat his response. "You would have us sit behind the walls acting as only cowards do? And what happens when they tire us out, poison our water and we exhaust our supplies... whilst their own supply lines from Siena remain open? Our women and children will starve, they will die slowly and they will die in the streets and the gutters. This is the course you would have us take? You know nothing of war; with your smart clothes and *pretty* face. When have you ever bled on the field of battle? What hardships have you endured?"

Clearly taken aback by the ferocity with which the large Swiss objected to his suggestions, Fabio Moretto swallowed nervously before steeling himself for his reply. "You would have me elaborate upon the suffering and hardship I have endured. Alas, I can with no certainty give you the answer you seek. I speak only for the people of Florence in this matter. Our walls are high, and thick. It makes sense to make the greatest use of them."

Urs shook his head in disgust. The room pulsed with apprehension before Gonfaloniere De Larosa spoke to break the silence. "My mind is made up. Having spent many hours deliberating over this, we cannot afford to waste any more time and I have heard enough. Our army is ready, and our enemy approaches; we shall march to war. Have the army form up to march within the hour. We shall meet the armies of Siena in the field and win a glorious victory!"

The wilds of Tuscany, summer, 1483

The warm summer winds gusted gently through the gully in which Giovanni and his two companions had been hiding. With as much courage as they could muster, the three adventurers rode out to meet the rest of the Sienese scout cavalry column. Their surcoats were marked with the black and white halved coat of arms of Siena that fluttered from a pole in that same warm breeze. It was not long before the three caught up with the main body of the scouting force, some thirty or so men strong.

Giovanni's heart pounded when he saw the group of men before him. Gripping the reins of his horse even tighter, he tried to act as nonchalantly as possible, avoiding eye contact and keeping his face as impassive as he was able. He fought the urge to place his hand on his sword, even though every instinct in his body screamed at him to do so. Glancing at his two companions quickly, he was aware that their body language reflected his, so he returned his gaze to the front of the column. Suddenly, a harsh voice barked at him from his right. "You there, why are you out of formation, and where have you been?" Before Giovanni could reply, another scout clad in light armour rode up to the sergeant, and spoke in a hushed tone.

By now, however, the three newcomers had begun to attract attention from other members of the group, in particular, Isabella. Her slender, feminine frame seemed at odds with the oversized armoured breast plate and greaves that covered her body. Several lingering, suspicious stares were directed at her. Sensing the confusion and with a wary look in his eyes, Giovanni took the reins of his horse and led it slowly and carefully to the rear of the column, beckoning Otto and Isabella with a look to do the same.

As they fell into line at the back of the column, Isabella muttered under her breath, "Well, here we are, with our heads firmly in the lion's mouth, now what?"

Replying as nonchalantly as he could, Otto murmured, "We keep our heads down and wait for the right moment to escape. It won't be long before they realise that our trail has gone cold, at which point, they'll likely double back, most probably heading for that ravine we hid in earlier. When that happens, we carefully move away from the rear of the column and make a break for Florence."

Another scout turned his head round at the trio and gave them a sideways glance. Otto, sensing the scrutiny, stopped talking. Seeing no obvious danger, the curious cavalryman looked away again, at which point, Otto continued slowly. "We're not that far now. Perhaps ten, maybe fifteen miles. The terrain, however, is incredibly rough going and hilly. It will hinder us greatly."

With a barely perceptible nod of his head, Giovanni re-adjusted the chin strap on the cumbersome helmet that hid most of his face and spoke quietly. "Let me remind us all that if we are caught trying to escape, at least one of us *must* successfully return to Florence to pass on the news. If we fail in this, the consequences will be dire and all that we have endured, all that we have fought for will be for naught."

As the grim words sank in the column began to move forward, slowly at first, but eventually, Giovanni, Otto and Isabella moved off, heading in the direction of freedom and safety.

Tantalisingly close now, Florence lay some twelve miles to the north over hilly and, on occasion near-mountainous terrain. Approaching a forest, a cool breeze blew. The temperature dropped and the hairs stood erect on the back of Giovanni's neck. Casting a nervous glance at Otto, he swallowed, unsure of what they might find lurking within. Taking a risk, Giovanni whispered under his breath, "This is not far from where we were ambushed. We should be ready to move if anything," he paused, "untoward happens."

As the column of scouts approached the forest fringe, the sergeant appeared to have a change of heart. Unsure whether to go on or to double back, the line faltered, slowing its approach. The air stilled, the birds stopped singing and an uneasy tension pervaded the atmosphere. At the head of the column, the sergeant called his aide to him and discussed what they should do. After a few moments spent deliberating, the column moved forwards, inching closer into the cool darkness of the trees.

Republic of Florence, summer, 1483

The Florentine army marched through the streets of the city. Their heavily armoured boots thudded in unison on the cobblestones as cheering crowds stood to either side of them. Women threw flowers at their feet, occasionally running up to kiss a lucky soldier.

Riding towards the front of the column was Gonfaloniere De Larosa in his finest robes of state and looking resplendent in ermine. He was flanked by Marti Urs to his right, and his standard bearer carrying the great pennant bearing the heraldic coat of arms of Florence to his left.

In front of them loomed the great southern gate, forty feet high and dwarfing everything around them; made of heavy oak, each required dozens of men to move them. On this day the sun hung directly over them casting a dramatic shadow over the gatehouse. De Larosa, not for the first time, questioned whether or not he had made the right decision; it almost seemed to him as though the entire situation were a real-life game of chess, with the lives of thousands of people at stake.

As he rode past the crowds of people lining the streets, the heavy weight of responsibility felt like the proverbial sword of Damocles above his head. Should he have listened to the dissenting voices and remained behind the huge, protective city walls, perhaps trying to wait the situation out and hope that some form of resolution presented itself? Or was he right in taking what was perceived to be the decisive and heroic course of action that would restore power to the citizens of

Florence after months of fear and intimidation by an unseen and unknown menace? Muttering a brief prayer, he turned to his aide and signalled the advance of his own personal guard.

Many hundreds of cavalrymen rode through the southern gate, forming up outside the city walls. The dust kicked up from the horses' hooves made it difficult for onlookers to see clearly, although eventually it settled as the cavalry moved into position and waited. The long continuous column of heavily armed and armoured foot soldiers equipped with pikes and spears, swords and maces, mercenaries and archers armed with sturdy bows, marched through the streets and out through the gates onto the plains outside the city, also. Joining up with the cavalry, they began to march south with tight, military efficiency. Only a token force of pike men had been left to defend the city along with a larger force of archers lining the city walls. For now, the citizens of Florence would have to look to their own defences should the unthinkable happen. And De Larosa prayed that it wouldn't.

The wilds of Tuscany, summer, 1483

The entire column of armoured Sienese scouts had, by now, plunged into the dark, foreboding periphery of the forest. The density of the trees barely allowed sunlight to penetrate, lending the place an oppressive feel. A cloying, earthy smell permeated the air. No birds sang, no sounds could be heard, and the dank forest floor muffled the sound of horses' hooves.

A quarter of an hour had passed and there was no sign of an end to the forest path. Not realising that he had been holding his breath, Giovanni exhaled as slowly and quietly as he could and allowed himself to think, albeit momentarily, that there was no threat, that they were now perfectly safe. As soon as that thought entered his mind, a single arrow aimed at one of the leading scouts zipped out of the gloom, penetrating his armour and burying itself in the unfortunate man's throat. As the mortally injured scout grabbed hold of his throat and fell from his horse with his lifeblood gushing from the wound, more arrows flew through the air burying themselves in their intended targets.

All hell broke loose as men charged from the undergrowth wielding a variety of weapons and screaming terrible war cries.

"Bandits!" cried Giovanni!" Taking a firm grip of his reins, he screamed. "This is our chance, stay with me!"

Needing no further invitation, Otto and Isabella followed his lead, fending off anyone who got within striking range.

Within a few minutes all three had managed to put some distance between them and the ensuing chaos of the battle. Riding hard along the tightly winding forest track proved difficult; on more than one occasion, Otto received a slap in the face from a low lying branch, but the chance to escape was sufficient reward in itself. After less than ten minutes of frantic riding, a thin shaft of light appeared in the distance indicating the end of the forest. The trio rode harder and faster than ever, seemingly free of their pursuers who were now busily fighting for their lives several miles behind them.

Bursting out into brilliant sunshine, the three riders put at least another half mile between themselves and the forest before slowing down to catch their breath. Panting, Isabella spoke first. "How far from Florence do you think we are? Seven, eight miles?"

Gasping for breath and with his legs aching from the strain of staying in the saddle, Otto stared at the horizon intently, looking for any familiar features that may give some clue as to how far away they were from real safety. "Maybe, as the crow flies, but as I said, the terrain will slow us down considerably. We need to get as close as we can before nightfall. We don't want to be out here after dark because either those bandits or wild animals or even the terrain will kill us off. One wrong step in total darkness on these hills could prove to be fatal."

Giving their lathered horses valuable moments of rest, Giovanni, Otto and Isabella made for the nearest hill to give them a commanding view of the surrounding countryside.

After several hours of riding through the uneven, hilly terrain, Giovanni, Otto and Isabella had successfully escaped the clutches of the Sienese scouts and hill bandits. Patting the neck of his horse, Otto stopped suddenly, his mouth agape, his ears and eyes straining. As Giovanni and Isabella were talking, Otto, gestured with his right hand. "Shh, both of you! Can you hear that?" Only yards from the brow of the hill now, Otto whispered, "There it is again. Can you not hear that? It's a sort of soft rumbling sound?"

Dismounting, all three got down on their stomachs and inched their way forward, wary of being seen. As they reached the top of the hill, they were greeted by an astonishing sight.

The wilds of Tuscany, summer, 1483

The plains several miles to the south of Florence were surrounded on three sides by gentle, sloping hills covered in grasses and the sporadic tree. During the summer, the air was full of birdsong, and animals grazed with little care beyond that of the ravenous packs of wolves that inhabited the area. It was on these plains that the armies of Florence now gathered, as the Florentine military commanders busied themselves deciding where to stage the decisive battle against the armies of Siena.

In his commander's tent, Gonfaloniere De Larosa, wearing full, intricately engraved plate armour, was in deep discussion with his advisors and aides. The sides of the tent were rolled up as fully as possible to reduce the stifling heat. Mopping his brow with a cloth, De Larosa pointed to the map on the camp table that showed the most likely route the army of Siena would take in its journey towards Florence. A narrow gorge lay at the end of the route closest to Florence.

"What about here? We could defend the entrance to the gorge that they must negotiate to get here. They won't be able to bring the full weight of their numbers upon us. We ought to be able to hold them there for days if needs be."

Marti Urs, the tall, broad Swiss condottiere interjected. "With respect Signor, holding Siena for days is hardly what the citizens of Florence have in mind. That only buys us time, not victory. We need to be absolutely resolute in the manner in which we conquer our enemy;

we must engage them in the field before this gorge and defeat them soundly."

Heads nodded in agreement, but before any more could be said, a cry from outside drew their attention away from their plans.

Following the direction of the shouting, De Larosa and his staff bounded out of the command tent to see three helmetless figures on horseback, clad in the heraldry of the city of Siena, riding directly towards them. Their approach caused quite a stir; several archers were already ranging them, their bow strings pulled back as far as possible, armour piercing bodkin arrows pointing at the riders. There was, however, something strangely familiar about two of the riders at least. Straining his eyes in the bright summer sun, De Larosa held his hand over his eyes, shielding them from its glare. A sudden, shocking realisation dawned on him. By now, more archers had lined up and had started to loose off some ranging shots, the arrows were falling a good distant short, but it was only a matter of time before their deadly armour-piercing tips found their target.

"Stop!" screamed Urs, as he too had reached the same conclusion as De Larosa. Rushing to meet the riders, both De Larosa and Urs ran as fast they reasonably could clad in heavy armour. Further up the hill and riding down towards the Florentine army, two of the three riders were waving frantically and shouting at their would-be attackers. The archers ceased their fire, the ground in front of the three riders punctuated by at least two dozen arrows. As they drew nearer, the features of Giovanni

Lascorza and Otto Baldwinson became recognisable. A less familiar, beautiful female rode between them.

Coming to a complete halt, the three riders dismounted and presented themselves before Gonfaloniere De Larosa and his staff. The young Lascorza bowed as he presented himself. "Signor Gonfaloniere, it is most agreeable to see you again. We have much intelligence for you and so little time to act. The circumstances are grave indeed, far graver than we could ever imagine in our worst nightmares. We must talk, at once."

With relief written clearly across his face, De Larosa embraced Giovanni before leading him by the shoulder back to his tent. "We'd given you up for lost, my boy. Feared the worst. Florence is in near turmoil. There was so little further news, and so little to act upon" said De Larosa.

"It nearly came to that, Signor," replied Giovanni with a glint in his eye. "We have little time, so I must inform you of all that we have learnt. The situation could not be worse; the life of every Florentine is in mortal danger. Pandolfo Petrucci is the mastermind behind all of this. He used Florentine merchants to broker deals with the Orient to collect the bodies of people who had died from the plague and bring them back here. Once those merchants learned too much, Petrucci had them murdered so that they would not reveal his intentions to the Signoria. He—" Giovanni hesitated, "had my father murdered also, believing him to be one of the few men in Florence capable of seeing through his deception. He ultimately seeks to annihilate Florence by unleashing a new bout of the Black Death upon us. Once this is achieved, his army will mop up whatever is left by laying siege and forcing entry into the city, then burning it to the ground. Thus, at one stroke, he removes Florence as his enemy and curries increased favour with the Borgia. He cares not about the wellbeing of his own men, for if he did he would not expose them to the pestilence in such a manner.

His hatred of Florence is great; it is *not* to be underestimated. As we speak, his army is on the march, no more than half a dozen miles behind us. I would estimate it to be at the very least an equal match for the army of Florence in both cavalry and infantrymen."

After listening to Giovanni's words, De Larosa knew immediately that they and Florence were now facing two deadly enemies. "Then we are caught between the hammer and the anvil it seems. Engaged here, in the field, with the forces of Siena we lack the numbers to face their army and deal with this death fleet approaching Florence. What to do, what to do?" he fretted.

"With your permission Signor, I think I may have a solution. If I might lead a small force back to Florence, I believe we can destroy the fleet before it has the chance to unload its cargo, while leaving you with sufficient numbers to complete your task here. I will take a force of archers to the west of the city and meet the ships with arrows before they reach it."

Taking only a moment to mull over Giovanni's suggestion and realising that there was little alternative, he consented. "Take a small force of archers and cavalry, infantrymen will only slow you down. Be swift though. If but a small part of that fleet makes the docks and delivers the cargo, all this will be for naught."

With a steely glint in his eyes, Giovanni nodded a brief bow in response and turned on his heels. Finding Otto, who had busied himself tending the horses, Giovanni explained what had to be done and set about gathering a small, mobile force to return to Florence.

Amidst the furore of the preparation for battle, and whilst listening to his young master, Otto knew that his skills would be better utilised in the field, facing the armies of Siena. It was while he and Giovanni were preparing the small force to return to Florence that he told Giovanni of his intentions.

"Giovanni, my place is here, standing in the line against Siena. Having seen your prowess against Petrucci's forces there is little more that I can do to support you. I believe I am needed here more than I am in Florence. As your aide, I would not leave your side without your unequivocal agreement; I do however, request your permission in this matter."

"I agree wholeheartedly old friend. However, I will agree to your request on the condition that you take the very best of care of yourself. I want no heroics on your part. An heroic, but dead, aide is of little use to me, or Florence. Is that understood?"

"I can but try, Signor," smiled Otto. "I would suggest, however, that you take Isabella with you if she is willing to go; it seems she can handle her own in a tight situation, and she may well be of more use to you than a slow, fat, old oaf like me." With a flourish and a bow, Otto turned away from his friend and walked off. After a few paces he turned back to Giovanni and said, "Signor, a mere suggestion, but you may wish to change from your current attire into something altogether more suitable."

And with a wink, he was gone.

Following Otto's advice, Giovanni changed from his scout's uniform into a suit of finest plate armour. The armourer that had marched with the Florentine forces helped Giovanni by buckling each armour plate in place with great care and diligence; finally a white surcoat bearing the red fleur de lys heraldic coat of arms of Florence was placed over the top of the armour completing the ensemble.

Whilst Giovanni had gone about equipping himself with armour and weaponry, Isabella had also finished debriefing the Gonfaloniere and his staff in the command tent. Astonishing the command staff with her level of detail and accuracy, the information that Isabella provided would ultimately prove to be invaluable for she alone had remained the longest in Siena. Painstakingly making notes of the troop types, their numbers and movements, she risked her life on a daily basis for a city that was not even hers. Her service to Florence had not gone unnoticed by the Signoria or the Gonfaloniere himself.

Walking over to Giovanni, Isabella raised an eyebrow and smiled. "Very fetching," she said. "I have presented my report to the command staff and Gonfaloniere De Larosa and in return they have informed me of your plan to return to Florence to eliminate the plague fleet. I wish to volunteer to come with you and Otto, if you will have me," she finished.

"Otto won't be coming with us; he's remaining with the army to lend his support here. He's right; this is what he does best. It's ultimately what he's spent a lifetime doing. Far be it from me to stand in his way and against his better judgement," replied Giovanni. "He did, however, recommend your services. Seems he's quite taken with your skill with the blade. You must've impressed him in Siena."

With a derisive snort, Isabella shook her head. "I think he was more impressed with you, Giovanni. He'd not have left you alone in this venture if he had not but the fullest of trust in you and your abilities. So, with that in mind, when do we leave?"

Giovanni pursed his lips, gave a shrill whistle and gathered together the thirty or so archers and cavalrymen who would return to Florence with them. In a tight circle, he told them of his plan.

The wilds of Tuscany, summer, 1483

It was with a great sense of dread that the sergeant of the scouting force returned to Pandolfo Petrucci; having returned empty-handed, he was not optimistic about his chances. The tyrant was notoriously short of patience when meeting with failure and was well renowned for his brutality in dealing with it.

Riding to within some twenty feet or so of Petrucci's tent, the sergeant dismounted and swallowed nervously before taking in a deep breath and entering the tent of the great tyrant. The tent was dimly lit and deep shadows cast their menacing aura about the interior. As the sergeant entered the tent, he allowed his eyes to adjust to the gloom. In the corner, he made out the form of a man clad in armour, seemingly deep in thought. Clearing his throat the master of scouts spoke in the darkness. "Sire, it is I, the sergeant of scouts. I have returned."

"Did you recover Lascorza and his aides as you were requested?" Petrucci's voice cut him off.

"No Sire, we did not. We'd lost their trail by the time we'd reached the forest before the plains of Greve. As we entered the forest, searching for them, we were attacked by what I can only presume were bandits. We were lucky to escape with our lives, less than half of our force remains alive."

A single, dreadful moment of silence passed, before being broken by Petrucci's voice. "So," he said very quietly, "you return empty-handed and with less than half of the men that I assigned to you? Is that the truth of the matter?"

Hesitating, dreading what was to come, the sergeant of scouts, replied simply, "Yes Sire,"

"And what of the armies of Florence?" growled Petrucci. "What did you make of them? Have you located their presence? What intelligence are you able to provide in this matter?"

Clearing his throat the sergeant replied, "We were unable to locate the armies of Florence, Sire. As I said, Sire, we made it as far as the forest before losing Lascorza's trail; having lost a great many men to the ambush by those bandits, we returned to await further orders and to recover our numbers." Terrified, his heart was now pounding in his chest, that pounding so loud it seemed to thrum in his ears; his mouth ran dry.

Petrucci sighed deeply, "So, in essence, you have failed to recover Lascorza and his aides and you have failed even to locate the armies of Florence. You allowed your force to be ambushed in a forest by mere bandits, many of your men killed, and you have the nerve, the gall no less, to return here, to me, empty-handed? Sergeant, you have been in my employ for some considerable time now, and as such you must be aware of the price of failure?"

Sensing the worst and with a feeling of utmost dread, the sergeant continued. "Please, Signor, you must give me a second chance. I can still be of great use and service to you and Siena!"

Petrucci, raising his right hand, before bringing his index finger to his lips, made a hushing noise to calm the man and his nerves. "I harbour considerable doubts about that, Sergeant. Your work here, for me, is done." With that Petrucci clicked his fingers twice. Hearing this command, two heavily armed and armoured guards pulled the tent flaps open illuminating the tent with brilliant sunshine. With the dazzling light shining directly in his eyes, the sergeant raised his hands to his face as the two guards' roughly grabbed hold of either side of him and dragged him from the tent kicking and screaming whilst begging for mercy and leniency.

With a sadistic grin, Petrucci shouted after them, "The price of failure in my service is not a second chance, but death in the foulest and most painful manner possible! You will serve as an example to others in my employ that success it its own reward!"

Outside, the sergeant, now weak from his struggling, was thrown to the ground with a bone-jarring thud. Striding from his tent, Petrucci stood over him. "Strip this man of his armour!" he demanded. "And get him to his feet. A soldier of Siena ought not die on his knees, even one so wretched as this!" he spat.

The terrified and now whimpering sergeant was dragged unceremoniously to his feet, openly shaking with fear.

"Behold! My thoughts on failure!" roared Petrucci, and with that he motioned to the guards who stood behind the sergeant. Grabbing a handful of the terrified sergeant's hair, the first guard yanked back his victim's head with considerable force taking the poor man off balance. In one fluid motion he drew his dagger and slid it across the sergeant's throat, the cold steel glinting in the summer sun as it passed from ear to ear. The second guard, somewhat gratuitously ran the already dying man through with his sword, the blade bursting from his abdomen. Gargling and spraying arterial blood in a fountain of crimson, the sergeant slumped to the floor, his life force spent.

Looking out over his gathered forces, Petrucci returned to his tent giving orders for his command staff to assemble. "Let us prepare," he said half to himself, "for the final onslaught!" Just moments later, as the tyrant's senior staff began to gather, a cry went up throughout the camp. "We've found them, we've found them!"

The wilds of Tuscany, summer, 1483

With his force of archers now assembled and riding as hard as they were able for Florence, Giovanni and Isabella placed themselves at the head of the small column. In the far distance, the glimmering towers of the walled city came into view. There had been several moments during the previous weeks when Giovanni had wondered to himself if he would ever see his home again. Now that he could see and almost feel her, he was very nearly overcome with joy. Grinning inanely, he pressed his horse even faster, desperate to pass through Florence's gates and end the madness that had been afflicting every free citizen of that beautiful city once and for all.

"We must head to the docks as soon as we reach Florence. If they land that cargo, all of this will have been in vain," cried Giovanni over his shoulder to Isabella.

"I think we should ambush them at the Ponte Vecchio, they'll have to strike their sails as the bridge will likely be too low to sail beneath; attack them there and they will be paralysed, unable to turn back and unable to make land. We can conceal some of the archers on the bridge itself and some on the banks."

Above the noise of the horses' hooves and with the wind rushing by his ears, it was hard to hear everything that Isabella had said, but Giovanni had heard enough to revise his original plan. "An even better idea, although we will need to gather more archers when we reach the city..."

Now the walls and gates of Florence were but a mile or so away and the standard bearer of Giovanni's force raised the banner bearing the coat of arms of Florence aloft, so that the men guarding the city walls would identify them without taking action against them.

They made the city gates moments later as the light began to fade, heralding dusk. Giovanni yelled out to the guards on the southern tower, "Open the gates! Open the gates in the name of the Signoria of Florence! I am Giovanni Lascorza in service to the Signoria, I have returned from Siena. Open these gates at once. I carry with me a message of proof from Gonfaloniere De Larosa, leading Florence's forces in the field; this scroll bears his personal seal of office!"

When this message had been passed to the gate commander, the order was given immediately to open the gates. Dozens of men ran to do his bidding removing the twelve-foot long reinforced oak bar before pulling back the great gates. The colossal wooden gates creaked as they opened, the entire process taking precious minutes, but Giovanni savoured every second, nonetheless. He had returned to his home city alive and whole and vastly more experienced than when he had left her protective walls some weeks before.

The gate commander, a man by the name of Michele Baccacio ran down from his vantage point on top of the southern gate to meet Giovanni and Isabella. "My sincerest thanks for your prompt response, Signor!" said Giovanni. "We have little time to explain. Suffice it to say that Florence faces a great threat from a fleet of ships heading this way; these ships must be destroyed at all costs. Our armies in the field are standing by to face

149

Siena. Signor, we must have as many archers as you can spare. If this fleet lands its cargo, we and all the other citizens of this city are dead. Do you understand the import of what I am telling you?"

Swallowing hastily Baccacio replied, "Of course Signor Lascorza. My men are yours to do with as you please, although we must maintain some semblance of defence along this section of the ramparts," he said pointing up at the nearby walls. "How many of my men do you require?" he asked.

"As many as you can spare, do you understand?"

With his now greatly augmented force of archers, Giovanni and Isabella raced through the narrow streets of Florence heading for the River Arno, all the while trying to arouse as little suspicion as possible so as not to alarm the local population any more than it already was.

As they neared the river, one of the archers cried out, "There, in the distance. I see them. I see the fleet!"

Looking to see where the man was pointing, Giovanni counted more than a dozen sets of sails. He and Isabella exchanged a concerned glance, the enormity of their situation made manifest for the first time.

They ran through the streets even faster as the huge enemy fleet sailed into view only half a mile from them. Now only yards from the Ponte Vecchio, the force of archers began to fan out, assuming defensive positions on either side of the Arno and on the ancient bridge itself.

"We'll need fire to really make this work," said one of the archers. "If we can set the fleet ablaze, the day is ours."

Giovanni gave the order to make fire; he was, however, painfully aware that it would take precious minutes to light enough small fires to supply the entire force, time that they sorely lacked.

Republic of Florence, summer, 1483

On the bridge of the command vessel, Captain Hai Jiang navigated his fleet closer and closer towards the heart of Florence with expert skill. The final stage of his journey was about to come to fruition and nothing would be allowed to stand in his way. For the first time in months, he allowed himself to dream of the riches he would earn and how he would spend them. In the short term, wine and women would suffice he decided.

As his thoughts wandered, he was brought back to harsh reality by his first officer calling to him. "Captain, there, on the banks, looks like archers, and on the bridge, too!"

Taking the proffered spyglass and cursing his luck, Hai Jiang decided to thwart his ambushers. "In that case, we have little option. We must make land sooner. First officer, bring the fleet alongside anywhere you see fit. I rather doubt we'll make it past that bridge in any semblance of strength."

The fleet altered its course, heading for the nearest suitable bank to make landfall. The ships had now become a hive of activity. Armed soldiers clambered onto the upper decks, ready to force their way ashore if necessary. Labourers and sailors began moving their deadly cargo, contained in black, sealed caskets, onto the upper decks; nothing was going to hold them up.

After many minutes, the fleet made an impromptu landing. Whilst orders were shouted across the decks of each of vessel in the fleet, the first wave of armoured men hit the marshy ground and ran forward taking up an outward-facing defensive perimeter. All dozen vessels had now dropped anchor and their disembarked soldiers had taken up defensive formations all about them, and, safely out of range of the force of archers stationed near the Ponte Vecchio, the sailors and labourers of the merchant fleet worked frantically, unloading the black wooden boxes off the ships, and onto the side streets of Florence.

"Come on, you vermin! Work harder! Get this foul devilry off my ships or at the very least it'll be the lash for you! God help you! If I don't get you, the Florentines will, and they'll be far less forgiving than I!" cried Hai Jiang. The captain, fully aware of the gravity of the situation, willed his ship's company to work harder and faster than they ever had before.

Isabella peeked out from her vantage point on the Ponte Vecchio and turned to Giovanni with a dismayed look on her face. "Damn it! They've seen us; they're making for the marshy ground to the south of the Arno! It's a game of cat and mouse now, Giovanni. A game that we can ill afford to lose!" she continued, her voice tinged with anger.

Leaning against the wall of the ancient bridge, Giovanni grabbed his bow and quiver, rubbed his chin pensively and passed the news down through the rest of the force that they had been spied by the enemy and that now, the onus would be on them to chase the infiltrating force through the narrow and winding streets of Florence. The implications of missing just one of the caskets containing the foul, lethal cargo of plague would have dire and dreadful consequences for the city and her populace. It was an all or nothing situation.

Sixty men and one woman now stood in the defence of Florence. Their efforts and actions would mean the difference between saving the lives of tens of thousands of people or the possibility of the worst outbreak of the Black Death in over a hundred years. The eerily quiet streets lent an tense atmosphere to the endeavour as the normally bustling metropolis lived in mortal fear of a besieging army to the south and strange rumours surrounding the murdered merchants.

Naturally, where there were gaps in the factual accounts, the terrified masses had filled them in with stories and hearsay. What began as the murder of a few men became far more sinister and stories of daemonic worship and debauchery abounded. Even though this could not have been further from the truth of the matter, the palpable terror the rumours caused led the citizens of Florence to remain locked in their homes, virtual prisoners in their own city.

With his men gathered around him, Giovanni spoke quickly and directly. "I counted a dozen ships, each with at least a dozen caskets on board, that should leave a minimum of seventy caskets to locate and destroy. However, we do have one thing in our favour; they won't be able to penetrate too far into the city as the caskets will be heavy and difficult to carry. If we establish a perimeter around the landing point and drive them back from there we might yet prevail. Those caskets must be burned to a cinder; it's the only sure way to eliminate the risk of contagion." Seeing many nervous faces around him, Giovanni continued bleakly, "The dead cannot hurt us brothers. Only the living can do that. Shoot the casket bearers first, and then secure the caskets; once you've done that, set fire to them any way you can. Fire your fire arrows into them then rip timber from anywhere, to make a good fire around them; it won't matter from where, if we fail in our task. These caskets are probably lead-lined. We have to melt the lead to get at the contents."

Dusk had long since begun to cast long shadows on the narrow streets. The cream coloured buildings and terracotta roof tiles had by now lost their familiar patina and had assumed a darker colouration in the dimming light. As night grew near, the prospects looked grim. In failing light, the small group of archers had to locate somewhere in the region of seventy caskets and kill their bearers without allowing the contents of those caskets with their dreadful corruption to spill out onto the streets.

"Giovanni, this will be like looking for a needle in a haystack," said Isabella. "If we happen to chance upon them in the dark then all well and good, but we cannot take any chances in these conditions. We simply have no idea how many of these things we have to destroy and where to even begin finding them."

Gritting his teeth and clearly irritated by his friend's words, Giovanni replied, "Isabella, we have little choice in the matter. We shall start with the streets that are adjacent to the river. Now, enough talking. We must be swift!"

The archers separated into smaller groups of roughly five men each before moving off into the fast encroaching darkness. One man in each group had lit a torch, the light from which cast grotesque, dancing, shadows on the surrounding buildings. Sprinting through the darkening maze, Giovanni's force made towards the last known heading of the invading force.

It was not long before the first contact was made. Giovanni and Isabella heard a man cry out, "Over there! I see them! Quickly!" One of the groups of archers had made contact with a small group of the invading force carrying their vile cargo and proceeded to let loose with their armour-piercing arrows. Very little time elapsed before the force of soldiers carrying the caskets had been eliminated.

Approaching the caskets with a mixture of disgust tinged with absolute fear, the archers loyal to Florence counted five caskets before setting fire to them with the aid of the torch they carried. Ripping tinder, dry timber, from a nearby fence they stacked it around the caskets enabling the fire to catch properly, sending sparks high up into the air. Shouting out into the darkness that they'd destroyed five caskets, their faint cries were heard from a street or two away. Accordingly, Giovanni produced a small piece of parchment and made a note of the number.

Isabella meanwhile, had led her small force towards the merchant vessels, determined that

156

whosoever lay behind this would not escape and live to tell the tale. Her group was larger than the others, with ten men at her disposal. Making their way through the winding streets, they stumbled across several armoured soldiers from the mercenary fleet. The surprise on both sides was noticeable as they'd effectively found each other in the darkness when neither force was expecting it.

With swords drawn, both sides charged each other, hacking and stabbing at will. Blood flowed freely in the streets and the cries of the wounded and dying terrified the inhabitants of the houses nearby. Removing her sword from the throat of the last soldier, it caught briefly in his breast plate; straining, Isabella pulled hard before withdrawing the blade and wiping away the blood on the man's kerchief. Fighting for breath, she whispered to the survivors, "We must be close; I think we have but to round that corner to the left, then straight on to the landing site. When we reach it, I want no distractions and no hesitation. Make every arrow count. Target their vessels with fire arrows; do not stop firing until you see that each ship is well and truly ablaze. The scum will pay for what they have done here."

She let her voice trail off, listening for any sounds that would signal the approach of further enemies. In the darkness, they moved with precision and speed, knowing the streets far better than their opposition. Before Isabella could count to fifty, they had reached the river, coming out of the streets and right beside the River Arno itself. Here the river ran slow but deep enough to grant even the largest of ships access to the port of Florence.

The enemy ships lay alongside the bank, line astern, their immense bulk blotting out the stars that were beginning to appear.

"We have the advantage of surprise. They ought not to be expecting an attacking force at this stage, but that advantage will not last long in all likelihood," whispered Isabella. Easing her face round the corner and spying the nearest ship, she gestured to the remaining eight men in her force to light their arrows. "Target the first ship. Light your arrows and unleash a hailstorm. Don't give them time to recover and do not stop firing until that first ship lights up the night sky. Once the first ship is well alight, we'll have to move to an adjacent street and continue working our way through the fleet, using the buildings as cover. Once they realise our numbers, they won't hesitate to attack. Does everyone understand?"

Not one man present questioned her right to command, the authority in her voice and mien evident to all.

Nodding, each man touched his respective arrows to the flame of the torch, and waited for the oiled wadding to catch fire. Deathly calm, they all stepped into view of the first ship, drew back their bows and unleashed a small hail of fire arrows onto it. Mere seconds later, a second round of arrows found their mark, followed by a third volley another few moments after that. In a matter of minutes the first vessel was alight, the spitting and crackling fires almost as high as the tallest buildings in the surrounding streets.

Casting a deep orange glow over the locality, the fire roared out of control. Shouts and screams of confusion, agony and surprise pierced the night as the merchant crewmen and soldiers reeled from the initial attack. Isabella and her force had, however, underestimated just how quickly their enemy would respond.

Knowing that their element of surprise was lost, Isabella and her small band tried to slip quietly away towards the next street. At the last moment, they were prevented from doing so by a large unit of enemy mercenaries who had spied their foe and were now charging headlong towards them. A hail of arrows from Isabella's men cut down the first wave, and a mass of soldiers collapsed in a heap having been pierced and stuck through by armour-piercing arrow heads.

"Fall back!" cried Isabella as the opposing force gathered in increasing numbers. Needing little excuse and relying strongly on their local knowledge, they began to fall back into the shadows, taking up positions in nearby alleyways, controlling their breathing as best they could, their hearts pounding in their chests.

The merchant mercenaries slowly spread out into the surrounding streets hunting for their prey, their weapons and shields held cautiously in front of them. The flames from the burning ship provided the slightest illumination behind them. From the darkness an arrow flew, penetrating the throat of the first mercenary. His gargled cries echoed in the silence and there was a look of sheer surprise on his face as he fell to his knees, feebly

159

clutching at the offending arrow in desperate futility. This arrow was followed by a hail of arrows with each one finding its mark. Men stumbled and flailed around in the darkness with arrows protruding from their faces, chests, and limbs, and once again screams of fear and anguish rang out in the night.

Falling back to the river, the mercenaries' courage failed them at the last. The prospect of advancing into near darkness with an entrenched enemy unleashing a hail of arrows into their ranks filled them with dread. Most had clearly joined up for a life of adventure; this much was apparent by the paths that each of them had chosen, but none of them in their right mind had anticipated just how dangerous this task would be.

This was precisely the stroke of luck that Isabella and her men needed. Seeing the retreat, they followed hard on the heels of the men who had only moments before been almost within touching distance. Gathering their wits, they ran swiftly to the river, assembled near a large plank of wood that was ablaze and continued with their initial mission of setting fire to the merchant fleet. All around them lay the dead, dying and injured enemy. The sailors and mercenaries who had survived the preliminary attack were desperately trying to confine the fire and prevent them from spreading any further, although a light summer breeze made that all but impossible. Luck, it seemed was on the side of the righteous.

Some distance away, Giovanni heard the cries and saw a huge orange glow coming from the direction of the river. The streets were bathed in an unearthly incandescence which lent an altogether eerie feeling to the proceedings. An overwhelming reek of smoke filled the air making it increasingly harder to breathe.

As he ran round the corner of the nearest street, Giovanni bowled straight into a casket bearer, knocking them both to the ground. As the other man fell he dropped the front of the casket which, landing awkwardly with a huge crash, spewed its contents out onto the street.

Immediately a vile stench hit Giovanni forcing him to cover his nose and mouth. Gagging and reeling in horror at what he saw in front of him he doubled over, willing himself not to vomit he failed and retched the contents of his stomach on the cobbled street. The putrefied remains of what was once, presumably a man, spilled out onto the cobblestones covering them in slime and decay. Almost fainting with the bile that had built up in the back of his throat, Giovanni was only dimly aware of a desperate duel that had broken out around him between his own men and the two casket bearers. Brief seconds later, the latter were dead, run through, while their shattered cargo lay on the ground.

Dragging Giovanni away from the casket and hauling him to his feet, his men had already begun the process of setting fire to the casket and its occupant. Only time would tell if any contagion had been unleashed on the streets of Florence, but there was little that could be done about that now.

Clearing his throat and spitting the last remnants of bile and vomit from his mouth, Giovanni regained his senses and carried on the task of making a note of how many coffins had been destroyed.

"Signor Lascorza, are you well? Signor Lascorza?"

Giovanni heard the voice of one of his men, turned to him and nodded. "I am well, recovered enough to continue. I thank you for your concern, brother. We must redouble our efforts if we're to win the night; that was too close," Giovanni rose to his feet and the group continued with their task.

For the next twenty to thirty minutes, sporadic shouts of success were called out into the stillness of the night, and on every occasion Giovanni was careful to note down the tally of how many caskets had been encountered and incinerated.

Coming to a crossroads, Giovanni heard a cry of surprise from behind him. Turning immediately to the source of the noise, he was greeted by the sight of one of his men being dragged into a nearby alleyway kicking and screaming before falling ominously silent. For a long, lingering moment, nobody moved, their heavy breathing contrasting with the still air that surrounded them, their swords were pointed expertly in the direction of the dark gaping mouth of the alley.

Suddenly from the darkness, five crazed mercenaries leapt, hacking and slashing at all around them. The clash of metal on metal rang out through the stifling night air as the two parties duelled to the death. Emerging from the shadows in front of Giovanni stepped a huge, muscular savage – oriental in appearance and sporting a large duelling scar running diagonally across the length of his weathered face. Standing several inches taller than Lascorza, he had a cold, cruel disposition and his hand fingered an intimidating cutlass. Barking orders at the other mercenaries in some foreign tongue, he clearly was there leader. Spying his opposite in Giovanni, he wished for one on one combat.

"I'd always been told men from the east were quite short in stature," Giovanni began.

A long sinister smile fell across the mercenary captain's face, revealing teeth like broken, yellow-brown glass.

"Clearly I was misinformed" finished Giovanni.

Both men cautiously circled one another, looking for an opening, a moment to strike. Seeing what he believed to be his chance, the grinning mercenary made a figure of eight movement with his cumbersome blade, slashing out towards Giovanni's torso. Parrying the blade in the nick of time, Giovanni kicked out in an attempt to sweep his opponents legs from beneath him and deliver a coup de grace. Chuckling at the somewhat clumsy move and believing himself to have the upper hand, the mercenary struck out again and again with brutal force. Longing for a shield, Giovanni was forced further and further back, his arms weakening from the bone shattering strength of his opponent's attack. Their blades locked momentarily as the mercenary powerfully surged forwards, confident of victory. His strength now failing him, Giovanni dropped to one knee as he struggled to maintain his defence; too little rest over too many days had finally taken its toll at the worst possible moment. With a sadistic grin on his face, the mercenary quickly sent a punch direct to Giovanni's jaw and, with the young man momentarily stunned, landed a heavy kick square to his chest – sending the beleaguered Lascorza sprawling to the ground. Dazed and heavily winded, Giovanni desperately tried to regain his footing, aware that on his back in the dirt he was defenceless; but he could no more find his feet than he could his breath. Wheezing in pain, he defiantly raised his sword – bitterly aware he could offer little opposition to the next inevitable strike. With mocking laughter the mercenary swung his cutlass, sending Giovanni's sword flying from his hand in one sweeping movement. Standing over the defeated Florentine with a look of triumph written over his face, the mercenary raised his blade for the killer blow; the moment seemed to last an eternity.

Determined not to look away but to face his fear, Giovanni looked up at his apparent executioner and spoke "Is this death?"

Suddenly, and from out of nowhere, a body came slamming into the side of the cruel mercenary, sending him crashing to the ground. So swift was the interception that it appeared as a blur and left Giovanni slightly stunned; expecting, as he was, a death blow from his opponent. Regaining his composure, Giovanni looked over to where his saviour and the mercenary were now struggling and was shocked to see it was Roberto Moretti – his bannerman – who had saved his life. Having seen his captain's dire predicament from a distance, Roberto, who was barely more than a boy, had sprinted hard to defend him. Summing up as much force as he could, he ploughed into the midriff of the ferocious oriental. Now grappling on the cobbled floor, they struggled for dominance but despite his best efforts, the young bannerman could little match the superior strength of the vicious mercenary. Desperately scrabbling to find his sword, Giovanni watched in horror as the ruthless savage produced a razor sharp dagger from its scabbard and drove it deep into young Moretti's heart, killing him instantly. Laughing mercilessly and standing over the now dead bannerman, the mercenary twisted the knife free and - with his eyes locked on Giovanni – brought the blade to his lips, licking the blood from the cold steel.

Something inside Giovanni snapped and with a roar he leapt to his feet. Despite the intense anger and rage that coursed through him, his mind was clear now – perhaps clearer than it had ever been. This barbarian that stood before him, this evil murderer, was the embodiment of Petrucci's Siena – wicked and cruel. Roberto Moretti's death would not be in vain, for his sacrifice represented the honour and quality of Florence, fighting to the end against tyranny. Giovanni realised that this was the moment of truth – for the person that emerged triumphant from this duel would lead his men to victory. The stakes could not be higher; if he failed, all of Florence would perish. Spying his sword beside his feet, Giovanni skilfully flicked the blade upwards with his boot, catching it dramatically in mid-air by the grip. Raising his sword to his face in a salute to his fallen comrade Moretti, Lascorza slowly extended his arm, pointing his weapon directly at the huge, brute before him.

Gesturing with his left hand for the mercenary to approach, Giovanni spoke. "Let's end this!" and with that, both men charged.

Exploiting the advantages of his smaller size and lighter blade, Giovanni swiftly side-stepped his opponents attack, appearing graceful and refined against the mercenary's clumsy movements. Flicks of his wrist were accompanied by the sound of slicing air – and flesh – as he cut the brute across the thighs and the back of his left knee. He was employing the techniques taught to him by both his father and Otto from many years before, the poetic justice that they were being used to save this great city was not lost on Giovanni. All the distractions of the battle had faded from Giovanni's mind. His focus was absolute. He would not fail his Florence.

Roaring in agony, the mercenary stumbled trying to regain his balance. Sensing victory, it was now Giovanni's turn to plant a heavy boot to his opponent's chest, sending him flying backwards and crashing into and demolishing a nearby wall. Cut and severely injured from the fallen debris, the savage somehow managed to rise, shakily standing despite bleeding heavily from multiple wounds. He turned and faced Giovanni in a last attempt to win the duel, swinging wildly with his fists aimed squarely at Giovanni's face in desperation.

"This is for Roberto Moretti you verminous scum!" shouted Giovanni as he plunged his sword into the mercenary's chest, all the way to the hilt. His face frozen and mouth agape, the mercenary gasped for a breath that would never come. Tearing his sword from the lifeless body in one motion, Giovanni stood panting with his lofted sword above his head and roared a victory cry.

Seeing their leader and champion dead, the few remaining mercenaries attempted to escape into the night but were cut down where they fled by the now superior number of Florentine soldiers.

Stepping from his slain foe, Giovanni raised himself onto the partially collapsed wall and, standing victoriously for all to see, he addressed the surviving soldiers. Noticing that around him the skirmish was over and that his men had won the night. "Brothers, you have fought with nerves of steel and hearts of honour! History will surely sing of your courage! We have lost our own this night, and there can be none who feel their loss more keenly than I. This ordeal is far from over, though; to the men who dragged me to my feet when I lost my senses at the sight of that plague corpse, I thank you. It will not happen again. To you who have fought by my side this night and bled with me, I thank you also. Without our sacrifice, our city stands no chance against this treachery. Now, I count that we have eliminated more than half of the suspected number of caskets. We have much yet still to do; into the night, brothers, into the night."

And with that, those who had survived thus far strode into the cloying darkness in their search for the deadly caskets that threatened to destroy all that they held dear.

Wilds of Tuscany, summer, 1483

For many long years now, Otto had believed that if a man needed something doing, it was better that he performed the task himself. It was this belief that occupied his thoughts as he sharpened his mighty two-handed blade, Gertrude, on the grind stone that he had been sitting at for almost thirty minutes. Bright sparks flew off into the night and provided an almost hypnotic element to his daydreaming. Equally, for many years, Otto had been a creature of habit. Before any possible or even probable military encounter, he had always honed and sharpened whatever weapon he used to its greatest point, believing that if he took care of his equipment, it would ultimately take care of him. Seated by his grindstone, with a small fire lit, he was interrupted from his private thoughts by a messenger summoning him to the Gonfaloniere's tent.

"Otto Baldwinson, you are," the messenger paused choosing his words carefully, "respectfully requested to attend a meeting in Gonfaloniere De Larosa's tent at your earliest convenience."

Smiling at the last part of the message, and its inherent meaning of, "you are requested to come immediately," Otto sighed, and carefully put his sword back into its scabbard and hefted it so that the point of the scabbard touched the floor. As he had his back to the messenger, he turned and replied, "You may inform Gonfaloniere De Larosa that I shall be there immediately, and that I am honoured that they should see fit to include me in their plans."

A curt and brief "Yes Signor, I shall inform them at once" was the only response.

Emitting a grunt of discomfort as he rose to his feet, Otto inhaled deeply through his nose and savoured the scents of the night. The air seemed clearer and calmer at night, especially in a military camp where the various blacksmiths and craftsmen did so much to pollute it during the day.

Night was a time that Otto had always looked forward to during his many years on campaign. It gave him time to think and ponder the issues of his life. Staring out into the darkness, he sniffed and walked in the direction of De Larosa's command tent. The thousands of camp fires all around the makeshift camp illuminated the way perfectly enough. Although many tents had been erected, many soldiers simply chose to sleep outside under the very stars themselves. Throughout the camp, men cheered and gambled, drank and argued, much the way it had always been since time immemorial.

Upon reaching De Larosa's tent, he presented himself to the guards that stood to attention outside. "Please inform the Gonfaloniere, that Otto Baldwinson has arrived at his request and wishes to add to his counsel," said Otto.

Moments later he was ushered into the large tent. Inside it was brightly lit with numerous candles and lamps. In the centre sat a great oak table upon which lay a parchment map of the local area. Around the table were the many of the support staff, military leaders and advisors and the Gonfaloniere himself.

"Ah, Otto, I'm very glad you could attend. We have interesting news which I'm sure you'll be eager to hear," said De Larosa pointing at the map before him. "This morning we deployed our scouts to the south and west of this location, and it seems that the armies of Siena are not far from here. We had hoped to be able to delay them here," he continued, pointing at the map, "but that will no longer be possible. We cannot, I think, avoid a pitched battle and at this stage there is no further news as to the situation in Florence. By now Siena must know our location and be preparing accordingly. There have been many suggestions presented to us tonight, I would hear yours old friend."

Rubbing the grey stubble on his chin, Otto thought about the options to hand and, with the experience and gravitas that he commanded naturally, he spoke. "It appears Gonfaloniere, that we have few options. We could run and hide in Florence, but we do not as yet know what we would return to or even, God forbid whether we even have our city to return to at all." Otto paused for effect, letting that last statement sink in, before continuing. "We have missed our opportunity to contain their army here at this place," he said, pointing at the bottleneck on the map that had formerly been suggested as a place to delay Siena and her armies, "and a pitched battle has as much do with the will of God as it does the conduct of its generals. On the face of it, it appears that our options are limited. However, I would suggest another possibility, if you would hear me out?"

With their curiosity clearly piqued, the men gathered around the table raised their eyebrows in surprise and listened with keen interest. With a wry smile, it was De Larosa who spoke first. "Signor Baldwinson, it is not like you to be so coy. You are amongst friends here, and as such you may share your ideas as you see fit."

A light ripple of laughter at De Larosa's gently teasing words emanated from the gathered aides and advisors.

Knowing full well that he was being gently teased, Otto smiled in return and raised his hands in mock offence. "Gentlemen," he continued. "I appreciate the humour, but I would suggest you hear what I have to say before making light of me."

Realising that it would better serve the situation if a calmer head was maintained, De Larosa raised his hands asking for quiet. "Forgive me Otto, I thought a little jest might go a long way, but you are right, perhaps this is not the right time. I meant no offence, please, continue."

"There was none taken, Gonfaloniere; you are right, we are in need of good cheer now more than ever, I would say. My plan is simply this: whilst we have the advantage of surprise, let us take a small force to their camp, in the dead of night and raze it to the ground. A light cavalry force will approach from each point of the compass. Their objective would be to make it to the centre of the enemy's camp and with torch in hand spread death, fire and destruction upon them. If we pull it off successfully, they, in all likelihood will lack the stomach for any further fight and will return to Siena with

171

their tails firmly between their legs. If they do stay to fight tomorrow, we will have the upper hand over their morale. Of course, I would volunteer to lead the assault, but I appreciate there may be others with greater claim than I."

A great furore rose up around the tent in a crescendo of noise. "It's too risky!" shouted one voice.

"It is a fool's errand that will surely end in the massacre of our cavalry! We cannot afford this venture, we should simply meet them on the field and be done with it!" shouted another.

A calm, but firm voice spoke out. "A bold and decisive plan, even if it doesn't work, it *will* hurt their morale and let them know that we have the edge over them. In fact, I like it so much, I will volunteer to lead the attack."

All eyes turned to the far side of the tent and there, in the shadows, was the imposing form of Marti Urs. The tumult died away as those gathered looked at Gonfaloniere De Larosa, wondering what his decision would be.

"Brothers, we have arrived at a point where no man should ever find himself – at war with a treacherous enemy and caught between tyranny and his city being destroyed by contagion. We ought to ask ourselves how we walked so easily into these circumstances, but those are questions for another time. Here, now, we have to decide only how to win the day and I firmly believe that we must explore any and all options, including the one presented to us by Signor Baldwinson. Therefore, it is my decision that we shall attack in the very midst of the night, and that the force shall be led by Signor Urs."

Turning his face to Otto, De Larosa continued, "Otto, I would appreciate having you and your wisdom by my side. I will require further planning assistance should this venture only be partially successful."

Nodding his consent, Otto, happy that his idea had been accepted, sat down and lit his pipe. Gonfaloniere De Larosa continued issuing orders. "Signor Urs, please make the necessary preparations for a small cavalry force to be equipped for this venture. Take forty men, ten for each point of the compass. That should be sufficient to cause enough mayhem in their camp; whilst leaving us with adequate numbers should we need to take to the field either tomorrow or in the days following. I want all metal muffled and be sure to wear something that will identify you in the darkness. I want no mishaps as a result of this. Death from enemy action is one thing; death from a lack of due care is unacceptable. The rest of us will continue the planning should the need arise. Does everyone understand what is expected?"

With a clear sense of focus, the group of advisors and aides nodded. "Good," continued De Larosa. "In that case, Signor Urs, you are dismissed; you may take any such men and materials as you see fit."

With a barely perceptible nod of his head, Marti Urs turned on his heel and walked out of the tent and into the star-lit darkness.

The wilds of Tuscany, summer, 1483

Gonfaloniere De Larosa called out across the tent, "Signor Baldwinson, I would talk with you about our odds for victory. Do you believe tonight's expedition will succeed in routing their entire army?"

Otto, feeling as though he was being put on the spot, looked around the tent, feeling the penetrating gaze of De Larosa. "It is my belief Signor that in time of dire need, men must have a clear goal to unite them, to give them hope and direction. This," he paused attempting to find the right word, "this mission, will give them that. If it goes to plan, I believe it will seriously dent the morale of the army of Siena, perhaps even cause a mass defection. At worst, our cavalry will have limited success, but still put the fear of God into them and give them a sleepless night. We must be on our guard, however, to ensure that the same fate does not befall us. It would be prudent to plan ahead for the morrow. If I may see the map, Signor?"

With a click of his fingers, De Larosa gestured to one of his personal attendants who quickly rolled out a more detailed parchment map of the area. The map was large, several feet across, and scorched and scuffed around the edges, suggesting that it had seen much use.

Still smoking his pipe, Otto rose up from his seat and walked to where De Larosa was now standing. With a careful and much-practised glance, he took in the vital information needed to plan the events of the following day. The aromatic smoke of Otto's pipe mingled with the scent of sweat and wine in the sweltering hot interior of the tent. After several moments' consideration, Otto pointed. "There. We should meet them there, the plains of Greve. The ground is flat; it will enable us to move effectively. It is protected on the left flank by this stretch of forest, whilst on the right lies the River Arno. Hit them tonight, and if they're still here in the morning, we'll lure them here. The rest, well that lies in God's hands. We should form up three lines of pikemen here, across the centre, supported by our swordsmen, our cavalry and knights on the flanks, and a reserve force of cavalry, here and here with our archers interspersed."

With a grim smile, De Larosa showed his appreciation. "Well met, Signor. Well met. I am profoundly glad that you elected to remain here with us. I just hope that all this is not for naught and that there is still a Florence here in the morning worth defending."

A mere twenty to thirty minutes after the initial meeting in De Larosa's command tent, the expeditionary force was assembled, briefed and ready to move out. A small force of forty cavalrymen sat lined up in twos, ready to march on the enemy camp and wreak as much havoc as possible. Each man was lightly armoured to reduce noise and to increase their chance of taking the enemy by surprise. Bits, stirrups and anything that would make a noise and give away their presence had been wrapped in cloth. Each man was also carrying unlit torches that, at the right time, would be lit and hurled into the heart of the enemy camp.

At the head of the column sat the imposing bulk of Urs himself; with his hand raised in the air, he signalled the force to ride out of the camp and into the night. Every man in the column had affixed to his upper left arm a knotted white piece of cloth to identify him to his fellow attacker.

Having decided to take some night air to reinvigorate him after the stress of military planning, Otto watched the column slip out of the camp. Taking in a deep breath, he sighed and wondered where the following day would lead him. With a worried frown, he turned his thoughts to Giovanni and Isabella and how their individual fates were intertwined with his own. Life had recently become rather complicated, and he yearned for a simpler, more straightforward time.

He was jolted from his private thoughts as a young messenger still in his teens brought him back to the present. "Signor Baldwinson, you are requested to—"

Otto cut him off with a kindly, tired smile, "Meet with Gonfaloniere De Larosa. Yes, forgive me; I was just taking some air. I'll come with you now. I'd just finished."

The Republic of Florence, summer, 1483

With an intense heat that could be felt from the side streets that ran parallel to the river, the fires on several ships raged uncontrollably. Sailors, soldiers and officers fought to maintain a semblance of order within the chaos that now reigned. A cacophony of noise ensured that orders had to be shouted to be heard, and it was in this madness that Isabella and the remnants of her unit now revelled.

No longer having to pass themselves off as merchants or soldiers, they walked fearlessly and calmly through the centre of the ruckus, casually dispatching those that ventured too near and helping spread the flames by starting further small fires along the way, wherever possible. Fire, smoke and heat raged all around them. It was an inferno that the great Dante himself would recognise, although perhaps not in his own city. It was in this inferno that the captain of the enemy fleet spotted Isabella. Like a vision, her image cast a stark contrast with all around her, and it was this that was to be her undoing.

"Who in hell is that whore's child?" he demanded. "Can it be that only I can see that she is the daemon here? I allow no villainous whores near my ships. Where are my archers? I want her head, whoever she is. I swear it! I will give a whole month's pay to the man that brings me her head!"

At that, a hail of arrows was unleashed at Isabella and her raiding force. The foremost man in Isabella's band noticed the volley first and screamed to the others to take cover. He was hit in the cheek for his trouble, the arrow penetrated cleanly through his face and out through his mouth. With a scream, he fell to the ground writhing in shock and agony, his face a bloody mess.

At the precise moment that Isabella sprinted over to help the stricken man, a heavy bolt flew straight and true through the air ripping through Isabella's shoulder and into her torso. Convulsing, she fell barely conscious to the cobblestones and lay there as blood pooled about her from her wound. Her mouth opened and closed in pain and shock. Her eyelids drooped as time slowed down, and Isabella's breath began to fade, coming in sharp, shallow gasps. From that fiery world, both she and her companion were dragged away to relative safety. Her final memory before fading into the cold, dark grip of unconsciousness was the concerned, frowning face of Giovanni Lascorza looking down upon her, and the terrible orange backdrop of a fleet of ships now ablaze.

"Move her carefully, damn it!" shouted Giovanni as the limp form of Isabella was dragged into the side streets. An arrow had pierced her shoulder and had lodged firmly in her upper torso.

"My lord, she cannot stay here. She must receive care for this wound if she is to stand any chance of survival!" replied a voice in the haze.

Giovanni squinted, struggling through the thick, acrid smoke to see who had replied. He recognised him as one of the men that had been with Isabella in their assault on the dockside.

Giovanni nodded and replied, "Take her to the infirmary near Il Duomo. We can do no good for her here. See that all that can be done for her is done. Do not forget to tell them that she has served Florence well and is a personal friend of the House of Lascorza."

With a heavy heart, Giovanni leaned close to Isabella feeling her faint, warm breath on his cheek. With one final gesture, he looked around him to ensure he was not being watched before placing a small kiss on her forehead. "Be well Isabella. Be well," he whispered.

Giovanni watched as the limp forms of Isabella and the gravely wounded archer were carried away to safety. He then turned to the remaining force, of which less than half were still alive or able to continue the fight, looking each man in the eye as he did so. "Brothers, we cannot win this fight by conventional means. By my estimate, no more than half of those caskets have been destroyed. It would take but one to wipe this city, our home, from the map. What I am about to suggest, will not sit well with anyone, but hear it you must, for if we fail to act decisively, all is lost," Giovanni swallowed before continuing. "We must evacuate this area of all its inhabitants, and burn this part of the city to the ground. It is the only way with any certainty that we can guarantee the removal of all taint of pestilence upon this place."

Astounded at the suggestion, the men around him responded angrily. One man cried, "Aye, we need not have feared the forces of Siena when we would but destroy our homes ourselves! I cannot agree to this, Signor Lascorza! There is folly and madness in what you are saying! At the very least, we ought to notify the Signoria of your idea. They would not respond kindly to having the city burned from under them without even knowing the circumstances!" Some just shook their heads in disagreement; others stared at Giovanni as though his words were heretical.

They, however, were not the only ones who were angry. Rising to his feet, furious at their unwillingness to follow him to the end, Giovanni looked at each man with contempt plain his face. "Do you think that this is a course of action that I contemplate with ease or something that I suggested lightly? To burn my own city to eliminate a far greater threat is not something I would do on a whim gentleman. Far from it, but I can see now that you are cowards, despite your actions tonight."

Each man hung his face in shame; the accusation of cowardice having stung them.

Lowering his voice to a calmer tone, Giovanni spoke in a gentler manner. "Brothers, we must finish this here. Destroy their fleet, evacuate this part of the city and burn the surrounding streets. Force them back to their ships and cut them down where they stand. I and I alone will accept the punishment for our actions. You are all witness to my testament. You are, however, right about notifying the Signoria. When we move the inhabitants of this area away from the fire; we shall send word to them."

Within minutes, the few remaining men were hammering at doors all about them, warning folk of the coming firestorm and telling them to hurry and pack what they must. Hundreds of citizens made their way towards the Ponte Vecchio Bridge, a bottleneck of souls forming at the entrance to the bridge. Women gathered small children in their arms; the elderly and infirm walked aided by sticks and the supportive arms of their family or loved ones.

The sight appeared to Giovanni to be sorry indeed. Wearied by many hours of action, and in need of rest and food, he and his survivors returned to the emptying streets surrounding the merchant fleet's landing site. "Each man will take a torch and burn anything at ground level that is flammable. Move towards the dockside in groups of twos and threes, each group covering their own street. Let nothing survive, neither cat nor dog," said Giovanni.

"And when we reach the dockside? What then? The city will be in flames behind us and we'll have nowhere to retreat to," said one of the more vocal men.

Giovanni replied succinctly, "Aye, and neither will they; there will be nowhere to run for any of us. There will be a reckoning."

As the import of his words sank in, the group scattered through the deserted streets, setting fire to everything they could. Oily smoke from the warehouses where fabric and wool were stored billowed up into the night sky, obscuring the stars themselves. It wasn't long before the flames grew higher reaching the very tops of the surrounding buildings that had stood for centuries.

The heat and smoke became almost unbearable. Coughing and retching, clutching damp cloths to their faces, the small force that had set out with Giovanni and Isabella to save Florence from threat now found themselves in the process of razing at least part of their city to the ground.

Having split into pairs or threes, each group now advanced on the dockside, laying waste to everything behind them. With that part of the city now burning fiercely, each group had assembled on the dockside where almost the entire fleet burned freely with just one or two ships partially ablaze and desperately trying to sail to freedom, lay at an awkward angle in the midst of the River Arno.

The wilds of Siena, summer, 1483

It was approaching the witching hour when the Sienese camp that had been asleep for hours came under attack. From every direction they came, hurling their torches and screaming insults. In their midst, a giant of a man rode flanked on either side by his own body guards. With their torches hurled at the nearest tents, they charged into the now burning camp with lance and sword cutting and hacking at everything within reach.

The guards surrounding the tent of the tyrant Petrucci burst through the outer canvas with desperate news. They found the tent in darkness for their master had taken to his bed the hour before. "Sire, Sire we are attacked! The enemy are upon us! The camp is in flames!"

Sitting upright, Petrucci blinked himself awake, before clutching his sword and strapping it to his waist. Racing out of the tent, the scene that greeted him was one of death and destruction. "Give me that!" he roared at his nearest guard gesturing to his spear. Immediately the spear was handed to him. Taking it by the haft with a firm grip, he levelled it at shoulder height and waited for the nearest intruder to venture too close.

Through the smoke, Petrucci made out the image of a huge man armed with a long lance, slaughtering his men with wild abandon. With a feral snarl, he hurled the spear as hard as he could. It flew through the air like a bolt, hitting, and almost skewering, the target through the midriff and dropping him from his horse.

The camp burned; perhaps as many as a hundred men or more had perished, and many others were wounded, but eventually the surprise attack was beaten off.

Striding over to the prone form of the man he had unhorsed, Pandolfo Petrucci grabbed the haft of the spear and twisted it savagely backwards and forwards. Groaning in terrible agony, Marti Urs, bleeding from his mouth, his eyes glazed with pain, spat a bloody insult in his native tongue.

Getting down on one knee and with his right hand taking a firm grip of Urs' head, Petrucci leaned close to the mortally wounded man. "I can make this easier on you, if you tell me that which I would know. Who are you and whom do you serve? Where are the armies of Florence, and what do you know of their plans? Speak and I shall make your passing swift. Hold your tongue and your suffering will be great, this much I promise you."

Urs raised his head defiantly. "My name is Marti Urs. I am the aide and right hand man of the Gonfaloniere of Florence, Piero Bartolo De Larosa. We came here to exact our revenge upon the enemies of Florence." Shuddering in pain, his mouth leaking blood from the great wound in his abdomen, Urs continued, "Our spies informed us long ago that you and your forces were up to great evil, it was just the extent of that evil which eluded us but now your merchant fleet is doomed to destruction as a force has been sent to eliminate it."

Petrucci grabbed the haft of the spear again, twisting it first one way then another. "Fool!" he roared. "Even if you should eliminate my fleet, my armies will crush Florence one way or another. The city you serve will perish and everything you hold dear, every idiocy of false democracy, every simple pleasure your merchant fleets provide for you will vanish, forever! Your home, your wife and children, your family and friends, everyone will die, I will see to that."

Allowing those words to penetrate, Petrucci continued, his voice now quiet but throbbing with malice, "Now tell me of the plans of your army."

Urs replied as calmly and as dignified as a mortally wounded man could. "Our armies will meet you upon any field of your choice at any appointed hour and win the day. Perhaps you could find your way to acting as a man just once in your miserable, worthless life and fight your opponent without resorting to hiding in the shadows. They will meet you on the morrow, that is, if you are man enough, which I wholly doubt."

The barbed insult was intended to goad Petrucci into an action that would present no clear favour to him. Being nobody's fool, Petrucci realised this and did not rise to the challenge. Instead he turned slowly to his attendant and said openly, intending all to hear him, "Make his exit from this world a long and painful one and then bring me his head. I have need of it."

Republic of Florence, summer, 1483

A truly apocalyptic scene greeted the citizens of Florence the following morning. Smoke rose from the ashes of a hundred or more fire-ravished buildings. Hundreds were now homeless; a few had lost their lives and many their livelihoods in the flames.

With a singed face, an exhausted Giovanni sat on the cold ground, barely awake. He recalled the events of the previous evening, reliving each memory vividly. Giovanni's men had so nearly been overwhelmed at the last moment, caught between the fires raging behind them and the savage fight with the enemy to their front. It was only when help had arrived in the form of armed men sent by the Signoria that they had finally won the day, capturing the merchant captain and forcing the surrender of his forces in turn.

Giovanni looked up at the form now casting a shadow upon him and squinted in the strong rays of the summer sun bearing down on him. "Can I help you?"

The messenger nodded solemnly. "Signor Giovanni Lascorza, you are hereby instructed to report to the Council of the Nine at the meeting chambers of the Palazzo Vecchio immediately. You will present yourself before the council and submit to questioning. Do you understand what is asked of you?"

"Of course. May I enquire as to why the council wishes to talk with me?" Giovanni replied with a concerned note in his voice.

"I believe, Signor, that they are most displeased at what they perceive to be the wanton destruction of

186

Florence. They do not agree with your assessment that it was the only way to ensure no disease was spread here. Forgive me Sire, I am but a messenger, but they have been most insistent. Your delay would only anger them further."

A resigned sigh was the only response Giovanni could give. Picking up his sword and wiping his face, he headed into the centre of the city, making for the Piazza Della Signoria. Walking through those that had continued about their daily business as though nothing had happened, Giovanni was struck by the speed at which people returned to their normal routines even in the face of the gravest of dangers and adversity. Street vendors sold their wares, children laughed as though no danger had ever been present, and life seemed much the same as it had been months beforehand.

Yet beneath the façade of normality there remained a sense of unease and dread, no doubt fuelled by the impending clash with the armies of Siena. If the forces of Florence lost on the field of battle, it would lead to a murderous and bloody siege. With barely enough soldiers left to garrison the city walls as it was, it was a siege that could have only once outcome.

A quarter of an hour later, Giovanni found himself standing outside the imposing, Palazzo Vecchio.

Making his way through the guards, Giovanni walked first through the open courtyard, before turning right up the marble steps and into the main meeting chamber. The council and all of its advisors and aides were present. Not for the first time, Giovanni found himself missing Otto at his side. Taking a deep breath and swallowing, he allowed himself to be ushered into their presence and was immediately greeted with a raucous interrogation of his previous night's actions.

Shouts erupted from the gathered group of the council and its advisors. "What in God's name did you think you were doing, man?" came one cry.

"He works for Siena! He has turned upon us!" cried another.

Despite all that he had recently endured, Giovanni had to fight to remain in control of his nerves. His throat now dry, he swallowed again, summoning up any last vestiges of courage he still possessed. Raising his arms to subdue those present, he made an impassioned plea. "I come before you not as traitor to Florence as some here have suggested, nor as a man possessed with the omniscience to know everything and every outcome. I do, however, come before you to defend my actions of last night. If you had been present, you would surely have agreed with my decision. Having personally encountered the contents of the plague caskets, my worst fears were confirmed that this was no elaborate ploy, but a serious and concerted attempt to sow the seeds of the Black Death in the very heart of Florence. To have allowed this would have been to allow the massacre of all that I hold dear, and that, I could not conceive of. If you think my actions reckless, meditate on how much more reckless it would have been for me to do nothing and allow those opposed to our fair city to wantonly spread death and disease. We had spent much time chasing down individual sources of this plague to little avail. I could not idly sit by and watch as my home was desecrated and my fellow Florentines were struck down by this vile pestilence. I did not have the luxury of a committee meeting, nor did I have the time to wait for a decision to come back from one. We had but one goal, to destroy those who would destroy us and to defend this city by any means possible. We were faced with defeat. We were faced with ruination. And we were faced with the prospect of Florence, our city, our home being wiped from the map for good. I was forced to act as I did, for failure would lead to consequences too great to bear."

Giovanni openly stared staring at various members of the assembled council.

A stunned silence filled the room, before a low murmur spread, chairs and feet shuffled awkwardly on the tiled floor as the whispering grew in volume.

"Signor Lascorza," spoke one voice, "my name is Fabio Moretto. I serve on Gonfaloniere De Larosa's staff as an administrator, and I speak for him in his absence. As you are no doubt aware, he is in the field, leading our forces against Siena. It is only by the grace of God, that the tenements and slums you razed to the ground were relatively isolated, or the entire city could easily have gone up in flames. Whilst I do not doubt that you believe you acted in the interests and the greater good of the city, you would do well to remember that you are *not* the Signoria, nor are you qualified to make decisions on the behalf of this city. Many here believe you acted with impudent recklessness and that your actions must not go unpunished. For my part, I will keep my opinions to myself, but this matter will be put on hold until the Gonfaloniere and our forces return, hopefully victoriously. Now, what is the status of the prisoners? I am correct in thinking that there were some prisoners captured from the enemy fleet, am I not?"

Pausing for a heartbeat and giving thought to his next words, Giovanni replied, "Signor Moretto, you are indeed correct, there were some prisoners captured. They sold their lives dearly to defend their captain, and we hold them in custody. There are roughly a dozen of them that still live. Some are gravely wounded, however. The captain of the fleet is also in custody. He is being held in solitary confinement. He may have much information to reveal. As regards your words about my actions, I have no shame in them and given the choice, would make the same ones again. You were not there, I was. There was too much of a risk that one casket would have remained hidden, the death and destruction that would've resulted from that, would have been catastrophic. If you wish to make me a scapegoat, then I shall not stand in your way. We shall, as you say, await the Gonfaloniere's return from the field and hear his words on the matter. Is there anything further that you wish to say?"

Walking to the front of the group, Moretto stopped mere feet away from Giovanni. Looking up, he said in a quiet, yet firm voice, "There is nothing further to add for now, Giovanni. You are not under arrest, but it would be most unwise for you were you to try and leave the city. It would send the wrong signal, shall we say."

With his eyes narrowed to slits, Giovanni leaned forward and whispered, "I have nothing to hide nor fear, and I have no intention of leaving my city, Signor Moretto." With no further matters to be discussed, Giovanni gracefully bowed and turned on his heel before leaving through the great meeting chamber doors.

Heaving a sigh of relief as he walked down the steps into the Piazza Della Signoria, his thoughts immediately turned to Isabella. When he had last checked on her, she remained stable, but her condition had not improved. Deciding to check on her again, he walked through the streets towards the infirmary in the heart of the city near the towering majesty of Il Duomo. The smell of smoke filled the streets and, in the distance to the south and west, Giovanni could still see the smoke rising from the previous night's actions.

Reaching the heavy wooden entrance to the infirmary, he opened the latch and stepped through into the building. Inside it was dark and warm and smelled of a heady mixture of potions and sickness. Allowing for his eyes to acclimatise to the darkness, he listened and heard the soft moans and groans of the patients as they called for help to any of the interns who would attend them. Walking through to the female wards, he passed various patients, the old and infirm and some of the people unintentionally caught up in the fires. He saw Isabella's bed and her almost lifeless form. The barely perceptible rise and fall of her chest was the only sign that she was still alive. Looking down to the wound in her shoulder, he realised that the barbed arrow head was gone, and in its place was a thick blood stained bandage.

Standing by the edge of her bed, he pulled up a small wooden stool and sat down beside her. Picking up the damp cloth near her bed, he carefully dabbed Isabella's forehead, wiping away the beads of sweat.

"Who are you? What is your business here?" asked a voice behind him.

Without turning to look, Giovanni replied quietly, "My name is Giovanni Lascorza; I am a friend of Isabella's, the lady that lies here. Are you one of her orderlies?"

"I am. The arrow was removed from her shoulder a little over an hour ago. She was barely conscious though, made almost no noise," came the simple reply.

With a gentle, resigned nod of his head, Giovanni continued in a strained voice, "What are her chances? Will she live?"

The orderly walked towards Giovanni and removed his cowl revealing a middle-aged, kindly face in the dim candlelight. "Young man, I can offer no such promises. Her life is in God's hands now. Her wound is grave although no arteries were severed. It has been cleaned and packed and that is about as much as we can do for her. Give her a day or two and we will have some clearer indication from there. I'm afraid that is all the assurance I can give you for now."

Smiling for the first time in as long as he could remember, Giovanni reached into the small leather pouch around his belt and took out a gold florin. "For your troubles?" said Giovanni.

The orderly placed his hand over Giovanni's and closed it. With a smile, he spoke. "I do God's work my son. That is reward enough for me." He turned and left.

Standing up from his chair, Giovanni leaned over Isabella's frail, prone form and kissed her on the forehead before leaving the infirmary. Walking out into the morning sun, his troubled thoughts were immediately drawn to Otto.

The wilds of Tuscany, summer, 1483

Roughly half way between Florence and Siena, in the midst of the rolling Tuscan hills lay the flat, featureless plains near the small town of Greve. Surrounding the plains on three sides were a great forest to the south and low lying hills that provided a tactically advantageous view of the terrain. The morning after the raid on the Sienese camp, the forces of Florence lined up in full formation on the top of a small ridge, facing south towards Siena. Hundreds of soldiers, mainly pikemen and swordsmen formed the central core of the army, their ornate and stylised armour glinting in the morning sun. On each flank lay a force of several hundred cavalry and behind them all, lay a large force of three hundred archers.

Ever since the first time he taken to the battlefield, Otto had been forced to contend with the nerves that threatened to overcome him; every man faced his daemons in his own way. Before each and every battle, he had always found a quiet and secluded place to meditate and make his peace with the world. That morning was no exception. In a small clearing in the nearby forest, Otto knelt in supplication chanting a mantra that he had used for as long as he could remember. "I am a warrior of God. In His faith, no harm shall befall me. With His strength to guide me, no enemy shall stand before me. With His guidance, my courage shall never fail me. Bathed in His light so shall my actions and deeds shine in His eyes." Otto paused. "Blessed be the Lord my God, who trains my hands for war and my fingers for battle."

Remaining silent for a moment in his kneeling position, he sniffed the moist earth. It gave him comfort, knowing that at the worst, he would return to it.

His meditation complete, Otto stood up, made the sign of the cross and walked over to his horse. He wore full armour, ornately decorated; over this he wore a thick, white, woollen cowl that covered his face and back. He mounted his large black stallion and walked the magnificent beast to the right of Gonfaloniere De Larosa, who was equally resplendent.

"There is no word of Signor Urs, I trust?" said Otto to the Gonfaloniere.

"There has been no word of him at all. One can only presume the worst; it is a great loss, both to the city and to me. He was a trusted aide and a good friend and confidante. There shall be a reckoning for this," said De Larosa sniffing the air.

Letting the words hang there, Otto looked out over the open ground in front of the army and recalled the last time he had felt nerves like this. Fighting a handful of opponents was one thing. Skill at arms could, and generally would, win the day; however, large, full-scale pitched battles were as much about good fortune as they were about anything else. The turmoil and frenzy of battle, hacking and cutting at everything and anything around you meant that life expectancy tended to be measured in minutes rather than years.

Taking a deep breath, he turned to De Larosa and spoke. "With your permission, Gonfaloniere, I should like to go and check on the men, make a final inspection."

De Larosa nodded, and Otto manoeuvred his steed to the right and rode down amongst the lines, relieved to be busy. His great sword hung from his back, and his armour enhanced his already prodigious bulk.

All along the line the pennants bearing the coat of arms of Florence hung limp in the still summer air. As if sensing the tension, the air was free of birdsong and the long grasses that shrouded the fringes of the plains were still. To the east, the sun had started to creep above the hills, illuminating the low lying flat lands. As he looked over the lines, making small talk with some of the troops, and going over the agreed plan in his mind, a commotion to his right caught his attention. There, in the middle distance, emerging from the forest, a helmeted man clad in plate armour bearing the halved black and white pennant of Siena against his left shoulder rode towards the Florentine lines on a dappled horse. In his right hand, he carried a hessian bag.

Riding to within arrow shot of the Florentine lines, the man stopped. Hurling invectives, the man carefully opened the bag and removed the contents.

To his horror, Otto realised that it was a human head. The decapitated head of Marti Urs, was grasped by the hair, the eyes having rolled back in his head, the tongue lolling from his mouth.

With a guttural laugh, the rider threw it towards the Florentines as hard as he could before removing his helmet and signalling to unseen forces behind him.

From the forest, the forces of Siena emerged. Slowly, but surely their numbers swelled. Archers led the way, providing cover, followed by thousands of sword and pikemen. Finally many hundreds of armoured knights sporting lances and sitting atop great destriers made their way towards the flanks.

Stunned by the strength aligned against them, Otto carefully made his way to the command group, and took his place alongside Gonfaloniere De Larosa. Both sides were now lined up immediately opposite each other. Neither side moved although horses whinnied and neighed; both forces simply stared at each other in silence for several minutes.

As Otto looked towards the opposing army, a small group of knights headed by Petrucci himself approached the Florentine lines. Raising his right hand and sweeping it forwards, De Larosa ushered his own group forward to meet Petrucci.

Mere yards apart the two groups halted. The silence continued, but Pandolpho Petrucci glared venomously at Otto. Eventually, he spoke, his sneering eyes still locked on Otto. "I do not parley with spies and the dregs of society. I ought to have known better that Florence, of all cities, would include lowlife such as you in their ranks."

Otto grabbed at the sword on his back only to have his arm steadied by De Larosa. De Larosa gave Otto a soothing look, followed by a barely perceptible shake of the head before turning to face Petrucci.

"Signor Petrucci, you would serve both yourself and the citizens of your city well, if you were to turn your army round and head for home. There need be no bloodshed here today. I feel obliged to inform you that your designs to wreak havoc upon my fair city have come to naught. As I am in a gracious mood, I will accept your apology and word, if you *are* a gentleman of course, that you will intend no such future actions. Failing that, I will endeavour to slaughter every last man here and a state of outright war will exist between our two cities. I ask you to consider these words and to think wisely."

A look of fury spread across Petrucci's face. "You *dare* threaten *me*? I have no need to listen to idle threats from you. Nor will I allow you to escape from this field alive. If our two cities are at war, so be it. You may consider that your answer!"

The strain in the air was unmistakeable. Otto drew his sword, hefting it over his shoulder and pointed it at Petrucci. "I shall make you pay for what you did to us, be warned. I shall find you on the field. You should know that your people despise you and will oppose you always, so long as you live."

Laughing, Petrucci replied, "If you are referring to your saviours that day, I am happy to inform you that every last man of them is quite dead. Their heads adorn my city's battlements as a warning to others. If you wish to find me, you have but to look," he paused, looking up at his personal heraldry. "Find my banner, and you shall find me. I look forward to meeting you again."

Both groups returned to their positions in their lines. De Larosa leant over to Otto and spoke quietly. "Otto, we now know that Marti Urs lies dead; I would ask that you lead the mounted contingent. It was to be his honour, but now that is no longer possible. I shall lead the infantry in the centre. The cavalry are yours to do with as you see fit. Do you accept this role?"

Embracing De Larosa in the warriors' grip, Otto simply nodded.

"Then let us continue," said De Larosa. "I pray to God that we live through this day; I wish you the best of luck Otto. Florence must stand, so let us get proceedings under way."

"Master of archers!" called the Gonfaloniere. "Stand by to let them have it. Take out their centre; hit them with everything you have. Is that understood?"

Wearing brown leather armour, the squat man who had served as the master of archers for many years now bowed and made his way back to his men. Otto moved into position at the head of the cavalry.

Moments later, the steadily growing breeze subsided briefly. Seeing the opportunity, the master of archers instructed his men to commence firing. Within seconds, thousands, of arrows flew through the air, their deadly trajectory tracing a line to the centre of the Sienese army. Arrows penetrated armour, pierced limbs and split faces and eyes, the blood flowed freely and men screamed in agony. The battle for Florence had begun.

199

Republic of Florence, summer, 1483

Water dripped from the moss and lichen-covered stone walls of the dungeons of Florence. Giovanni's thoughts returned to the last time he had spent time in a dungeon. His feet made soft padding noises as he walked further and further down into the very bowels of the city prisons on his way to visit their most important prisoner. Torches hung from the walls in sconces casting a dull glow that added to the brooding and claustrophobic nature of the place. Stopping when he reached the lowest level, he beckoned for the nearest of the guards to open the cell that contained the man he had come to see. The guard obligingly removed the keys from his belt and unlocked the heavy bolted door.

Recoiling briefly at the stench of the dungeon, Giovanni stooped to enter the low door and descended a small set of steps into the presence of the merchant fleet captain.

"To what do I owe the pleasure, Signor Lascorza, isn't it?" sneered Captain Hai Jiang.

Allowing his eyes to adjust to the darkness of the dimly lit dungeon, Giovanni could make out the captain sitting on a makeshift bed, nursing his wounded shoulder. "I am here to question you and I require answers. Moreover, the Signoria requires answers, and they will not be as lenient as I. It would be to your advantage to cooperate fully. If you do, I may have the power to make your passing swift and painless. If you do not assist, I will pass you to the Signoria, who will surely torture you for any information you may possess. I urge you to make the right decision here. There is no hope of escape or rescue; as we speak, our forces will likely be engaging Siena in the field. The only thing you can control now is how you exit this world."

"And what would you have me reveal were I to be interested in your most gracious of offers?" replied the captain, his voice dripping with sarcasm.

"I wish to know exactly what happened, who approached you to do this, when and how much you and your fellow mercenaries were to be paid. You will then tell me if there were any others involved in this plot. You will also tell me what you know of the Florentine merchants who were murdered. Were they in on the plot?"

With a derisory snort, the captain began his tale. "I was approached by various agents of Pandolpho Petrucci some six months ago; I only met him once. At this stage he informed me of his desire to obtain as many bodies that had succumbed to the plague as could be reasonably carried.

I found him to be an enigmatic man, full of flattery and deceit. He knew well, however, that in the Orient there are still sporadic outbreaks of plague and that bodies would not be difficult to obtain. At this stage, I swear to you I had no idea of his full intentions. Those he revealed later when we were too heavily implicated in his plot to extricate ourselves. We were to be paid the princely sum of five florins per body. A veritable fortune as I'm sure you can see, although I doubted we would receive any payment, and as such I could not bring myself to trust Petrucci. However, to his credit, we received a third of the payment in advance, with the remainder to be paid once our task was complete. Consequently we did as he asked and secured as many bodies as we could from our home lands.

After we had the bodies, he revealed his true intentions to us. Many of my men were already unsure about continuing on this errand. Those that found it too distasteful left my service, only to be captured by Petrucci's forces and brutally executed. He tolerates no dissent, and his word cannot be trusted.

Some two to three months ago, we made contact with several merchants in Florence with whom we wished to engage. We believed that we could reduce the risk to us and use them to bring the deadly cargo of plague caskets into Florence. Some of them got wise to the plan and threatened to speak out unless they received a larger share of the profit. Three merchants were murdered although there was a fourth man, not a merchant exactly, but a Florentine who sought to overthrow the Signoria and establish a new ruling class in a decimated and weakened Florence, one ripe for the taking. He still lives, I believe."

The hairs on the back of Giovanni's neck stood up and his blood ran cold as the full implications of what the captain was telling him hit home. He managed to speak before his voice cracked with emotion. "There is a fourth who lives? Tell me what you know of him, his name, what he looks like?"

"I cannot!" roared the captain. "I know not what he looks like! I was unsure of his existence until only relatively recently. It appears that he attempted to curry favour with the Gonfaloniere in order to exert a greater influence over proceedings. As to his name and what he looks like, I cannot help you there. I am truly sorry, but I cannot."

With a troubled frown, Giovanni spoke. "I thank you for all that you have said Captain Jiang; I shall inform the Signoria that you have been most helpful." Giovanni stood up remaining hunched over in the cramped confines of the cell.

"Wait, Signor!" called the captain. "You are a man of honour, I believe. Perhaps you could attempt to see if I might be pardoned in all of this?"

Looking away from the captain and turning his back, Giovanni replied, "I cannot promise anything. Your fate lies with the Signoria."

Leaping up from his seated position, the captain winced as his shoulder caused him pain. "But you said you could at least make my passing painless, that there would be no torture, is this a lie also?"

"Forgive me Captain, I had to get the information I needed from you one way or the other. For my deceit, I apologise."

The captain slumped back against the wall again before muttering under his breath, "Ha! The evils of men are easily masked with false flattery and charisma. In this way you are no different to Petrucci."

At the door, Giovanni paused and spoke one final time to the captain. "You who would oversee the death of an entire city for money *dare* speak ill of me? You shall reap that which you have sown."

As he left the small, dank cell, Giovanni's head reeled from what he had been told. At the heart of the matter, a spy acting contrary to the greater good had managed to gain some considerable influence within the governing body of Florence itself. To what end, he did not yet know.

Gleve plains, summer, 1483

For the second time that morning, the sky darkened as hundreds of arrows were unleashed; this time, however, it was the forces of Florence who bore the brunt. Scores died where they stood, their death cries piercing the air; many more were wounded, suffering horrific injuries. Not waiting for another volley, Gonfaloniere De Larosa signalled the general advance.

Several thousand Florentine soldiers and mercenaries advanced slowly towards the enemy, whilst the forces of Siena seeing the Florentines on the move, responded in kind. When both lines were twenty to thirty yards apart, they charged, slamming into each other with such force that men were knocked from their feet and crushed into the churning soil. The sound of sword meeting sword rang out across the battlefield, heads, arms and legs were hacked off with wild abandon and men on both sides slipped and fell in the blood and gore

Moments later the battlefield bore more than a passing resemblance to a butcher's shop, except that here, the cadavers were human and the price was paid in human lives.

The first wave of pikemen crashed into their enemy, skewering each other; the savagery and violence from both sides was enough to shock even the hardest of souls.

Otto had by now formed the Florentine cavalry into one large formation, hoping to smash the Sienese forces wherever they were at their weakest. Observing the slaughter that now took place in the centre, he raised his right hand and signalled for the cavalry to take a prominent position on the left flank. Glancing over his shoulder, Otto saw the Gonfaloniere, easily identified by his banner leading his elite unit into the immediate centre of the Sienese army. "He's mad!" muttered Otto to himself, vowing to keep an eye on him.

Immediately, the right flank of the Sienese army withdrew to reveal several hundred armoured knights armed with lances twice the length of a man. With no time to plan or react, Otto had but little choice and ordered the charge. The ground rumbled with the sound of hundreds of armoured knights on a collision course. Seconds later the first wave of opposing knights met, their lances took a terrible toll as they either knocked their enemies from their horse or tore through plate armour as if it were paper, causing grievous wounds or instant death to the owners.

As the main forces expended their lances, the fight became a close-quarter sword battle; there was little but providence to differentiate those that lived from those that suffered terrible deaths at the hands of their enemy. After a few moments of total bloodshed, so much choking dust from the plains had been kicked up that it was nigh on impossible to tell friend from foe; confusion reigned and in that moment, Otto viewed the great tyrant himself. He immediately changed course and charged for Petrucci who was still surrounded by his personal bodyguard. Sensing an opportunity to bring matters to a swift end, Otto rode past a spear that was stuck in the ground, and grabbed the shaft firmly. With a flick of his hand he deftly manoeuvred it into a position ready to throw. Some forty feet from Petrucci, Otto hurled the spear with all of his strength but at the very last moment, one of Petrucci's bodyguards threw himself into the path of the spear and took the brunt of it in his chest knocking him off his horse where he was immediately trampled by the melee all around.

Gritting his teeth and cursing his luck, Otto shouted out for support over the din of the battle and continued riding hard towards the small group surrounding Petrucci. Drawing his two-handed sword at the last second, Otto swung it with such ferocity that the nearest Sienese knight was smashed from his horse, breaking his neck on the hard ground below.

Time slowed, his heart raced and adrenaline pumped as Otto was overcome by blood lust. Roaring a mighty battle cry, he fell upon Petrucci's innermost bodyguard, his now deep-rooted hatred for the tyrant spurring him on. Supported by other Florentine knights now, a savage dance of blow and counter blow heralded a new level of desperation as both sides vied for dominance.

Overhead, ominous grey rainclouds formed. Cutting his way through several knights, Otto was now little more than twenty yards from Petrucci. "Coward!" roared Otto. "Your lies and deceit have caused the deaths of thousands, and for what, so that you may die, here in the mud a verminous wretch?"

As he spoke, Otto failed to notice the Sienese knight to his left thrust his spear at Otto's horse. The horse hurled Otto with such a force that he landed, heavily winded, crumpled in a heap, his armour battered and dented in numerous places. Tasting the rain that had begun to fall on his lips, Otto, through his dazed vision saw the cruel form of the great tyrant ride over to him, his lance aimed directly at Otto's heart.

Petrucci lowered his lance and roared his contempt. Otto moved his bodyweight and grabbed hold of the lance, flinging it over his shoulder and hurling the tyrant of Siena off his horse and into the dust now made mud by the amount of blood spilled. Grabbing the dagger at his belt, Otto frantically struggled over to where the prone form of Petrucci lay, and clambered onto him, wrenching the ornate helmet from his enemy's head.

"You are responsible for the death of my former master and friend. You were nearly responsible for my own death and that of countless others and your time is at an end!" he spat. Raising the dagger, Otto thrust it down with all his considerable might into the gaps between the plate armour.

Twisting his face in agony, Petrucci grabbed Otto's right wrist and tried to wrest it away. "*Lesser* men deserve all they get, *fool*!" panted Petrucci. "You and your kind are meaningless to me. The glory of Siena and *my* rule will stand above all others and there is nothing that you or any other man can do to prevent this."

"I beg to differ!" shouted Otto. With his gauntleted left hand, Otto struck the tyrant in the face breaking his nose and cutting a savage gash on his right cheek. "That was for my master, and this, this is for me,"

Otto ripped the dagger from the wound in Petrucci's chest with a growl and was about to thrust it back in again, when a knight loyal to Petrucci and Siena rushed towards him, striking him about the head with his mace.

For the second time in a matter of minutes, Otto found himself stunned. It was testament to his strength and sheer will, and the quality of the helmet and the chain mail that he wore beneath it, that he had not been knocked entirely unconscious. Blinking his vision clear, he saw Petrucci being dragged to relative safety behind a wall of armoured knights. Desperately trying to get to his feet, Otto realised that he had lost his dagger in the confusion. He staggered to his horse to find his trusted two-handed sword.

All around him death and brutal injury were being dispensed with little care or thought of the human blood being shed or the women left without their menfolk and children their fathers.

Fending off attacks from various quarters, Otto found a riderless horse. Still dazed, he mounted it and made his way closer to the Florentine lines. As he reached the bulk of the Florentine soldiers, he heard a great cry of despair. Turning in the direction of the noise, his heart sank as he realised that the Gonfaloniere was at the heart of the battle. From his mounted vantage point he saw De Larosa fall as he was struck in the face, his banner dropping into the mud.

With their leader downed, the Florentines in the centre began to waver, their hearts and minds becoming fearful and full of doubt. They broke and ran; leaving De

Larosa's bloodied body lying in the mud along with the banner of Florence.

"With me, now!" Otto roared over the clamour at the nearest group of Florentine knights. Half a dozen them charged into the swirling fray with Otto leading. Heedless of the risk to his own safety, Otto and his small entourage slammed into the nearest Sienese soldiers with such force that their front ranks were knocked senseless or crushed beneath the weight of their huge armoured destriers. With his comrades forming a protective circle around him, Otto dismounted and grabbed the body of De Larosa. With a superhuman effort Otto heaved him up onto a spare horse before remounting his own and riding towards the safety of what remained of the Florentine lines.

"You!" shouted Otto to the nearest Florentine knight. "Recover that banner; it must not fall to the enemy! *You* are the standard bearer now, understood?"

The brutish form of the knight nodded before he hurled himself into the enemy and recovered the standard.

"Fall back and regroup! Fall back and regroup!" Otto shouted until there was no further breath in his lungs and his voice was hoarse.

Petrucci's army pushed ever forward until a full cavalry attack into the Sienese centre temporarily halted their advance.

Otto continued riding behind the lines and into relative safety before quickly glancing behind and checking on the condition of De Larosa. Blood poured from an open wound on the Gonfaloniere's head, his nose appeared broken, but it seemed that he still drew breath. Otto handed De Larosa over to the chirurgeons and their assistants attached to the army before re-joining the fray.

The battle drew to a stalemate, and a little more than two hours later with their energies and anger spent, the battle came to an end with thousands of casualties. The dead and wounded lay on the field and the soft, pitiful groans of the dying was inescapable. Limbs and heads littered the ground and the soft marshy ground was thick with gore and blood.

With the casualties and dead collected, the Florentines began their arduous journey north, towards the safety of the great walls of Florence.

The snaking column of soldiers, more than a mile long, trudged along the muddy road that had formed after the rainfall. The men were exhausted, sore; many were wounded. At the head of the column rode Otto and the noblemen and senior mercenaries that served Florence; they were in no better condition.

A nobleman riding next to Otto took the chance to question the Germanic condottiero. "I hear Gonfaloniere De Larosa has sustained grave injuries, my Lord Baldwinson. You are the next in the chain of command. Are we to renew the fight with Siena?"

Otto was jolted back to reality at the question as his mind had wandered after the battle. He looked at the young nobleman that had spoken out and answered with the only words he could find. "There is little more we can do now. We shall return to Florence, lick our wounds and ponder our next move, I daresay. There were no winners here today, young man. Many ordinary men lost their lives today and for what, I'm not yet sure. I'm not sure I have the stomach for this anymore; this is the only thing that I can say with any certainty."

The knight interrupted him, "But why would Siena seek war with Florence. Who would gain from such a thing?"

Shaking his head Otto replied slowly, "There is a small minority of men who will, in some way, profit from all of this. Petrucci may well be one of them, but he must surely have had assistance in this matter. Do not underestimate the influence of power, greed and the lust for more, that corrupts men's souls."

"Forgive me, my Lord, I do not understand, more what, precisely?"

"Simply *more* than that which they currently possess, greed is the source of many of the world's evils. Greed corrupts every man if left unchecked, greed and a desire to control those around him."

"And that's what you think is the case here?"

"I cannot say for any certainty. I would not be surprised, however, if it were the case. Now, let us have no further talk of this. We shall arrive in Florence by dusk. I would suggest that you tend to those in your care and prepare them for their return."

The knight nodded his head before taking his place further back in the column.

Otto returned to the thoughts that had perplexed him previously. Who stood to benefit besides him? What would happen next now that a declaration of open war existed between the two cities? Otto's mind grew weary of the endless questions. Blinking his eyes and taking a deep breath through his nose, he glanced at the hills in the distance to his right and again wished for simpler times.

Republic of Florence, summer, 1483

Waking up in her small rickety wooden bed, Isabella immediately flinched in pain. Barely remembering the arrow head that had struck her in her left shoulder she reached over to feel the wound. She could see little as the candle at the side of her bed had almost burned itself out, but she sensed she had been sorely wounded. She smelled little but sickness and death and instantly longed to leave the infirmary in which she had been recovering. Sitting up and swinging her legs over the side of the bed, she stood, swaying, and took a few steps.

Seeing her movement, one of the attendants gently took hold of her right arm and tried to return her to her bed.

"Take your hands off me!" Isabella hissed.

"My dear girl, it is for your own benefit. You require rest and time to recover from your wound. I personally have been asked to pay particular attention to you by order of the Signoria themselves and also from someone who, I believe, is a friend of yours, my Lord Giovanni Lascorza. I could not, in all matters of good faith and conscience, ignore their will and allow you to leave this place until you are fully recovered."

Relenting, Isabella slumped back down into her bed but said nothing.

With a smile, the intern bowed and walked away.

Confident that he had left her to her own devices, Isabella sat up and once more got out of bed, regretting it almost immediately. Feeling unsure on her feet, she slowly and silently made her way to end of the corridor that led to the stairs to the ground floor and the heavy oak door.

The wooden floor creaked as it bore her weight. Instinctively, she stopped and allowed a brief second to pass before continuing on her way, listening out for any signs that the intern had returned. Eventually making it to the door, she slipped out of the infirmary and onto the streets of Florence.

Dusk was approaching and a large crowd of people rushed past, jostling her, making their way towards the great southern gate. Shielding her injured shoulder as best she could, she slowly, painfully, made her way against the run of the crowd and headed north into the heart of the city to the Palazzo Lascorza. Eventually, from vague references made to her by Giovanni, she found the palazzo and hammered at the gates to be let in.

The men that stood guard for the Lascorza family, surprised at her presence, immediately admitted her entry and notified Giovanni. Rushing to the gates, Giovanni took a firm, but gentle hold of Isabella, supporting her weight, before helping her to sit on one the benches in the courtyard.

"Isabella, this is madness. You ought to be recovering from your wounds. What are you doing here?" he said.

"There was no recovering from wounds to be done in that place. I was surrounded by death and disease. I beg you to let me stay here, Giovanni. I would ask you not to deny me that."

With a gentle, sympathetic smile, Giovanni replied. "There is something you should know, Isabella. The morning after the night that Florence burned, Otto and the forces of Florence engaged the armies of Siena in open battle. The reports are mixed. I do not think that the engagement was conclusive for either side, but I do know that Gonfaloniere De Larosa was gravely wounded, and his senior aide, Marti Urs was captured and killed. The army returns to us as we speak."

Swallowing heavily, Isabella replied, "And what of Otto? What news of him?"

Shaking his head, Giovanni said, "Of Otto, there is no news. It was my intention to meet the army at the southern gate. Are you up to travelling?"

Despite her wound, she gave a small, wry smile.

Giovanni's expression changed and he now frowned at Isabella. "There is more that you should know. The captain of the merchant fleet survived his captivity. I had chance to talk to him earlier. He revealed the truth and it appears that there is a spy, someone working within the Signoria, someone who has been working in tandem with Siena all along. I do not yet know who it is, but I am wary as to who to trust within the Signoria; I trust only you, Otto, and perhaps the Gonfaloniere himself. There is no way of knowing who is trustworthy and who the snake in the grass is. To think that one of our own would betray his fellow citizens for money; I can think of nothing worse."

Shaking her head, Isabella replied, "There is nothing worse, that's why. The mercenaries that are

216

employed as our protectors do so openly, for the most part. This, this is something else entirely. Do you have any idea at all who it can be?"

"No, the captain of the merchant fleet didn't even know, and he had liaisons with three merchants from Florence, all of whom were executed when their usefulness came to an end. The fourth however, still lives and must be found and made an example of."

"I have no doubt that when that day comes, they will be made a full example of. For now, we must meet the army at the southern gate, find Otto, and inform the Gonfaloniere."

"Agreed, but first a quick change of clothes. I think my sister may have something that will suit you. And we will find some food for you."

Republic of Florence, summer, 1483

Gathering in their thousands, the crowds lined the streets near the southern gate. They had cheered at first until the hundreds of wounded marched silently and solemnly through the great gates, their broken forms revealing the true horrors of war. Then the expressions on the faces in the crowd turned to shock and pity.

Giovanni and Isabella pushed their way through the crowds towards the head of the column and spied Otto. Breathing a sigh of relief, Giovanni shouted from the crowd and waved his hands in the air. "Otto! Otto!"

Looking to his left, Otto spied the younger man and, for the first time in days, smiled broadly despite his bruises. Giovanni gestured for Otto to leave the column and join them. Seeing the look in his master's eyes, Otto turned to the nobleman to his right and made his excuses before leaving the column and following Giovanni and Isabella into one of the narrow side streets that lined the route from the southern gates to the centre of the city. Thirty yards into the street, Otto dismounted from his horse and embraced the other two. His armour was dented in a dozen places and his face was covered in numerous cuts and abrasions.

"Tough fight, old friend?" said Giovanni.

"Aye, it was. The Gonfaloniere was wounded. He seems to be stable, but it was a closely run thing. In the end, the battle was indecisive. Petrucci still lives and I was unable to finish him when I had the chance. I was this close, Giovanni," said Otto holding his forefingers together for emphasis. "This close! I had to rescue De

Larosa, too. He led the centre and was almost surrounded. I saw him and the banner fall. It was all I could do to rally enough support to recover his body and the banner. Thank God that he still lives!"

"Otto, there is much to tell you and very little time. The threat here has been eliminated. The fleet made landfall and planted numerous caskets in the streets surrounding the southern docks and in the end there was little choice for us but to burn that part of the city and the caskets with it. To say that this did not ingratiate me with the Signoria is an understatement. In fact, they have forbidden me to leave the city as I appear to be under surveillance. Isabella herself was seriously wounded and is still recovering, but there is no time for that either. I had chance to speak to the captain of the fleet that carried the plague caskets, and from what he said, there is a spy working for Siena within Florence, within the Signoria itself."

Taking this information in and eying Isabella and her wound, Otto cleared his throat before continuing hoarsely, "This becomes more and more incestuous with each passing day. I can only presume that your situation with the Signoria will need all the support it can get. I am entirely grateful that the Gonfaloniere lives."

Shaking his head in incomprehension, Giovanni questioned his friend. "I don't understand, Otto. Why?"

"Giovanni, my boy, I saved the Gonfaloniere's life. For that, he owes me a favour, I should say. Whilst he is still the voice of this council, he will have much sway over them. I wouldn't worry about them, for now, at least."

"That still leaves us in a predicament. Just who we can trust in the Signoria? How long before De Larosa recovers from his wounds? We need at least one powerful, trustworthy ally on the council."

"In that case, we need to ensure that De Larosa survives. Although he is stable now, it would be in the interest of whoever this foul infiltrator is to see that he dies from his injuries. I suggest he recovers somewhere safe," replied Otto.

"Agreed and understood. Perhaps the Palazzo Lascorza would be appropriate in this case," muttered Giovanni.

A week had passed since the Florentine army had returned from the field, and in the safety of the Palazzo Lascorza Gonfaloniere De Larosa was on the way to recovery.

"Signor De Larosa." The Gonfaloniere was sitting in one of the upper chambers overlooking the courtyard. The scent of roses and lavender infused the warm summer air with its heady scent. "Signor De Larosa," came the voice again.

Straining and turning round in his chair, De Larosa smiled as he recognised Giovanni. "Signor Lascorza, it is most agreeable to see you. You are looking well. I understand you managed to avert a disaster in Florence by taking some rather decisive, but perhaps drastic, action. I also hear the Signoria are less impressed than I. Never fear, I shall use my power to gainsay them."

"Thank you, Gonfaloniere. I am most grateful for your support. However, there is something else that you should know." Ten minutes passed during which Giovanni explained to the Gonfaloniere that Petrucci had, at least according to the confession of the merchant captain, some form of assistance within Florence in arranging the entire set of events.

"But how do we know we can trust this merchant? He is, or at least was, on the side of Petrucci," mused De Larosa.

"I thought the same thing initially. He has no reason to lie to us, however. He knows he will not live. He knows his destiny lies on the hangman's gallows. In short, he has nothing to gain from revealing this information. With respect, I do not think we can afford to take what he has told us lightly."

Staring intently out of the window, De Larosa gritted his teeth. "So, only by the grace of God have we managed to fend off two attacks from a known enemy only to find that we still harbour a daemon in our midst. We are now in a state of war with Siena; this is a distraction we can ill afford, Giovanni. I cannot go in front of the Signoria and inform them that there is a traitor in our midst, on the say so of a captured enemy. We will need to conduct our own investigations, although quietly. The people need, no crave, stability. Not a word of this is to go beyond the walls of this palazzo. I presume Otto and Isabella are aware?" quizzed De Larosa.

Nodding, Giovanni replied, "They were the only ones I could trust implicitly. Besides..." Giovanni stopped in his tracks. "What if we could get the traitor to reveal himself?" said Giovanni excitedly.

"If we could do that, Giovanni, then we would save ourselves an inordinate amount of trouble. But how? No man in his right mind would simply admit that he is the traitorous canker at the heart of this devilish plot!"

"I have a plan, Gonfaloniere. I need the prisoner brought before the Signoria at once. Are you well enough to face them?" asked Giovanni.

"I am sufficiently recovered enough, thanks to your gracious care. What would you have me do?"

"I need you to gather the Signoria together, today, now. I also need you to double the guard at the Palazzo Vecchio. Bring Otto and Isabella with you. Meet me there in one hour. Also, if this works, I will need you to pardon the merchant captain."

"Giovanni, it is a lot that you ask of me. I can see my way to everything, but the pardoning? He intended to murder thousands of innocents for coin."

"Gonfaloniere, if this works, the merchant captain could flush out our quarry. The least he would deserve for his assistance would be a pardon."

With a resigned look on his face, De Larosa acquiesced. "I give you my word; you shall have what you need."

Rushing through the cramped streets, pushing his way through the crowds, Giovanni headed towards the city prison clutching the scroll bearing the great wax seal of the seat of Gonfaloniere of Justice. "Let me pass. I am here on urgent business of the Signoria and the Gonfaloniere of Florence. Let me pass! Stand aside!"

The guards at the city prison gates looked at each other cautiously before allowing Giovanni through the huge gates. As Giovanni entered the prison, he grabbed a torch and headed deep down into the lower levels where the most dangerous of prisoners were usually kept. By now, he knew the route well, and in a matter of minutes had made his way down to the merchant captain's cell. Presenting the guard outside his cell with the scroll bearing the seal of the city, Giovanni signalled for him to open the heavy door. The guard fumbled with the keys on his belt before finally opening the door to the dimly lit cell. Stepping inside, Giovanni could make out the form of the captain lying on the makeshift bed.

The merchant sat upright. "You… Have you come to gloat?"

"Silence!" hissed Giovanni. "We haven't a moment to lose. I'll explain on the way. You are to accompany me to the Palazzo Vecchio at once."

Republic of Florence, summer, 1483

Half a mile away, the limping form of the Gonfaloniere walked in tandem with Otto and Isabella towards the main entrance of the Palazzo Vecchio. With twenty guards marching in unison behind them, they made their way into the palazzo itself, through the initial open courtyard, past the fountains, and up the stairs that flanked the entrance into the second courtyard. As they walked up the stone staircase, Otto whispered, "I hope we know what we're doing."

Hearing this, De Larosa cast him a nervous glance before nodding slowly. "As do I, Otto. As do I." As they rounded the corner, they walked into the grand meeting chamber of the Palazzo Vecchio with its high ceilings and walls adorned with the work of the finest painters. Huge marble statues lined the edges of the chamber and in the centre, the Signoria had assembled, eager to see their Gonfaloniere who had remained an elusive figure since his return from battle.

"Gonfaloniere De Larosa!" cried several council members, as the small company walked into the chamber. The gathered crowd rose to their feet clapping and cheering their approval. With a beaming smile, De Larosa and his companions walked into the centre of the chamber. He seated himself comfortably, and Otto and Isabella took seats behind him. The guards that accompanied the Gonfaloniere remained outside of the chamber at his behest.

"Signors!" called De Larosa. The cheering and clapping continued. "Please… Friends… I implore you. The import of what I am about to say will at best shock you, at worst, well, there is no simple way of stating this. There is a traitor in our heart. A man so vile he has at every stage of the way aided and assisted Siena. His motivation, I suspect was little more than money and power." At that moment, De Larosa nodded up at the viewing gallery, signalling the next stage of the plan. "Unfortunately for the traitor, he did not count on one thing. My Lord Lascorza?"

Giovanni walked into the grand chamber; following him was the bedraggled form of a man, unshaven, dirty and with a dirty blood stained bandage binding his shoulder. The gathered council gasped audibly at his presence. Scanning the council for any sign of betrayal, De Larosa continued, "The penalty for treason is surely death by the foulest means." Allowing the gravity of his words to sink in, De Larosa resumed his carefully rehearsed address. "The prisoner is a high-ranking official in the employ of Siena. He will now reveal the traitor to us!"

Giovanni accompanied the merchant captain to the large rectangular table in the middle of the chamber from where they began to walk up and down before each council member and their associated staff. "If you will, Signor, please reveal to us now, the man who has betrayed his home and all we hold dear."

Many began to shuffle uneasily in their seats, voicing their concerns, but for one man it was all too

225

much. Fabio Moretto leapt to his feet in a blur, rushing for the exit, his face wide-eyed in terror. "Guards!" yelled De Larosa. "Arrest that man!"

Moretto bowled into the nearest guard as hard and as fast as he could, knocking him to the ground, but the guards were too numerous, too strong and too heavily armed for him to evade. Moments later, Moretto had been subdued, yet he continued to scream and protest as he was bound in chains and ropes. "Take him to the city prison, double the guards assigned to him. I want no mistakes. He will pay dearly for his treason! Understood?"

The sergeant of the guard saluted smartly before leading Moretto away to the gaol.

"How did you know it was Moretto?" De Larosa asked Giovanni quietly.

"I didn't. I simply wanted to try and flush out the spy and at the same time see if anyone reacted to the face of the captain. Either we found our spy, or we proved that the captain was lying to us. There was the chance that the spy wasn't present, or that he was such a calm character that he'd not reveal himself to us, but it was my belief that when enough pressure was applied in one specific moment, his hand would be forced. Thankfully and luckily for us, he did."

Stunned, De Larosa whispered into Giovanni's ear, "That was *some* gamble, Giovanni. Next time, please inform me of all the facets of a situation before I go in front of the ruling council of this city and potentially make a fool of myself. That aside, very well done. You ought to be aware, though, that you will have made powerful friends, but also equally powerful enemies. I should watch your step in future."

Smiling, Giovanni replied, "I'd have it no other way, Gonfaloniere De Larosa."

Returning the smile, De Larosa moved away from Giovanni and stood in front of the Signoria. "It seems that disaster has been averted. Florence has been damaged, but we shall recover. A state of war now exists between our city and Siena. These are trying times and we must pay attention to our enemy, for they will be sure to try to discover our weaknesses. In spite of all of that, I believe that a public ceremony of thanks and celebration would be the best way to express the gratitude of the good folk of Florence. If there are objections to this, please voice them now."

Not a sound could be heard in the vast high ceilinged meeting chamber.

"Excellent, then it is decided. A night of public of festivities, song and dance! The Signoria shall make the necessary arrangements."

Giovanni, upon hearing the news, smiled and walked over to where Otto and Isabella now stood. "It seems the mystery of the murdered merchants is solved. Who would have thought that a plot so sinister, so shrouded in intrigue would have led to the infiltration of our government and have taken us to a state of war?" said Otto.

"A month ago, life was so very simple, but now I can't quite see where my place is in the world," said Giovanni quietly.

Placing a consoling, fatherly arm around his shoulders, Otto replied, "You must be optimistic, my boy! Your father would be proud of you, of that, I am certain. Besides, you have me in your service and employ, what more could you want?"

Slowly, a grin spread across Giovanni's face. "For that, I think you can buy me a flagon of ale, Otto Baldwinson!"

"What about me?" said Isabella indignantly.

"Don't I deserve some ale too?"

Republic of Florence, summer, 1483

Two nights later, thousands had gathered to celebrate in the Piazza della Signoria and the night sky was filled with stars. A display of fireworks imported from the Orient crackled and fizzed overhead whilst musicians played the lute and minstrels sang. A great fire had been lit in the centre of the Piazza della Signoria where food was being served as a gift to the poorer people of the city.

The citizens of Florence had gathered in their finest clothes to relax, socialise and to simply enjoy the moment. Until recently life had been full of uncertainty and the threat of invasion had weighed heavily on the hearts and minds of the people. Now that the threat had been eliminated, the certainty and joy of life had returned to the city once more despite its now scarred appearance.

Wearing a dark blue overcoat made of the finest silk, Giovanni looked out over the celebrations below from the balcony on the side of the Palazzo Vecchio. Behind him, he heard padded footsteps. Casually glancing over his shoulder, the sight of Isabella in a dress of cream and pale blue silk greeted him.

"Why are you not down below enjoying what is, at least partially, your celebration?" she enquired shyly.

"I... I do not know," Giovanni stuttered in reply. Secretly Giovanni knew full well. The news that Isabella would be returning to Venice had simultaneously surprised and saddened him.

Isabella continued, "I came to say my goodbyes, Giovanni. Meeting you and being of assistance to Florence was liberating, to say the very least, but as you are aware, I received news this morning that my father is ill. I am sure that you, of all people, would recognise my need to return home. I'm not even sure I shall reach him in time, or just how grave his illness is. I wish there was another way."

With a weak smile, Giovanni placed his hand gently on Isabella's face. "You ought not to fret about it. I'm certain he will be fine. It is surely a temporary ailment that, with the right treatment, will clear up in no time at all. What will you do when you return home, to Venice?"

"I shall no doubt work for my father's textile business, a suitable line of work for a woman. You would agree, no?"

Raising his eyebrows, Giovanni chose his words carefully, yet retained a playful smile on his face. "Signorina, I'm not entirely convinced of that. Perhaps you'd be more suited to being a wealthy nobleman's bodyguard? Maybe you could become a mercenary?"

Pretending anger, Isabella placed her hands on her hips and narrowed her eyes to slits.

Interrupting the moment, Otto walked out onto the balcony. "What are you both doing out here? You should be down there, where the feasting and dancing is! Giovanni, we are to be publicly honoured tomorrow morning outside the Palazzo Vecchio at three hours past sunrise. I have just now been informed by the Gonfaloniere's staff." Pointing at Giovanni, Otto continued with a beaming grin, "It seems you are to be especially honoured. You have been rewarded with a public position of some standing and an annual stipend. What say you to that?"

With a wink, Giovanni gave his answer, "I am both honoured and flattered. I shall have need of an aide, I think."

"Of course, I know just the man!" replied Otto laughing.

With that, the three adventurers walked out of the palazzo and into the open courtyard to join in the merriment below.

Shortly after dawn the following morning, resplendent in his newly repaired armour, Otto walked towards the door to Giovanni's bed chambers in the Palazzo Lascorza. He knocked three times, waited a polite moment, and then opened the door. He walked over to the shuttered windows and opened them, allowing the early morning sun into the room. "Good morning, Signor. Time to rise! Today is the day of your public honouring by the Signoria. I have already made preparations for your clothes. The servants will wash you in the bath house on the ground floor,"

Rubbing the sleep from his eyes, Giovanni sat up slowly in his bed. "What happens now, Otto? Where do we go from here?"

In a fatherly tone of voice, Otto stood at the end of the large, ornate bed in which his young master now sat. "We do whatever our city asks of us. We go wherever the winds of fate lead us, and never shall we complain about the ride. You are young, wealthy and possess great skill, but you have much to learn about life; however, as I have pledged to you before, you will always have my sword, my support and my friendship, for as long as you require it. Now, get up, get washed and get dressed. We're due in the Piazza della Signoria within the hour." Otto bowed, and turned on his heel and walked out of the bed chamber.

Thirty minutes later, a clean, immaculately dressed Giovanni went out into the courtyard of the Palazzo Lascorza where Otto and Giovanni's sister, Cordelia were waiting. "Best not to keep the crowds waiting, Giovanni. You look pretty enough," remarked Otto.

Giovanni laughed heartily and took hold of Cordelia in a warm embrace. "We should leave then, Otto, old friend. Cordelia, you will come, won't you?"

"Of course!" she replied. The trio walked towards the gates of the Palazzo Lascorza, and out into the street. A warm sunny day beckoned. The sky was already a lustrous azure blue. The crowds had begun to gather and a great cheer erupted from the throngs as they caught site of Giovanni.

"Where's Isabella? It doesn't feel right without her here," asked Giovanni.

"She said she would meet us at the Piazza della Signoria at the allotted hour. Don't fret, young one. It serves no purpose," replied Otto.

As they turned the corner, they walked past Il Duomo in all its magnificent splendour, the breath-taking architecture of its polychrome marble panels glinting in the sun. The huge bells in the tower hundreds of feet above them rang out in celebration, and people leaned out of upper story windows to cheer and throw confetti.

"It's all rather overwhelming!" shouted Giovanni to Otto and Cordelia.

"It's magnificent!" replied Cordelia, shouting at the top of her voice to be heard over the din of the crowd.

Passing through the Piazza Del Duomo, they now had to force their way through the crowds as they approached the Piazza della Signoria.

"It's them! It's Lascorza!" cried some of the crowd.

"Saviour!" shouted others.

Women leapt at Giovanni and kissed him. Some even kissed Otto, much to his secret enjoyment.

Forcing their way through their many admirers, they eventually arrived in the Piazza della Signoria. A long, crimson carpet led up to a huge dais that had been erected in the centre of the square. On either side of the carpet, were trumpeters that sounded their shrill notes as Giovanni and Otto approached. On the dais stood De Larosa clad in full ermine cloak and backed by the entire Signoria. On the steps to the dais was Isabella smiling shyly and positively shining in the bright sunshine.

"Citizens, freemen of Florence, we are here today to pay homage and honour the deeds and actions of a young hero, a man of Florence, a son of Florence. In times of tyranny, those who stand up to be counted against seemingly insurmountable odds and are willing to pay with their lives in the service of the betterment of

233

humanity are those who will one day lead us to freedom. When we cower in our homes, we would do well to remember that there are those among us who will never bow down to power-hungry madmen," De Larosa paused, looking out over the thousands that now surrounded the dais. "We are privileged to have these people in our presence at this moment. Signor Lascorza, Signor Baldwinson, and Signorina De Franco, I extend our heartfelt gratitude to you. The end times may one day strike down our fair city, but not today and not whilst you are here," Choking at the sentiment, Giovanni made to speak only to be cut off by De Larosa. "It therefore gives me the greatest of pleasures to bestow the honour of knight and envoy of Florence upon you, Signor Lascorza. You shall represent this city in all matter of manners and affairs. You shall represent the best of us and speak for us in the absence of the Signoria. You shall carry this ring as a symbol of your office, and with it, your seal of state. It is a position of great responsibility."

Dumbfounded, Giovanni cast a nervous glance at Otto, unsure of how he should respond. "I am not entirely certain what to say, except that there is no need for gratitude, or honours. I did the only thing that I could in the service of my city. Service was its reward, I can assure you; I shall, however, accept everything that has been bestowed upon me with warmth and the utmost of pride. Thank you."

At that, the crowd roared its approval, and Gonfaloniere De Larosa took Giovanni by the arm and raised his hand into the air.

A week after their honouring, Giovanni sat with Otto and Cordelia in the courtyard of the Palazzo Lascorza, Isabella having returned to Venice. The sun shone, the warmth of the day began to gather, insects buzzed, birds sang, and Giovanni was deep in reflective thought.

"I'm wondering, has it sunk in yet?" said Otto. "The day is won; the enemy at the gate is thwarted, at least for now. We have carried out investigations into a series of murders, travelled to Siena, fended off bandits, joined the Commedia dell 'Arte, escaped from the clutches of our foulest enemy, fought pitched battles and almost burned down half of Florence. Now that you are envoy of our fair city, there will be much travelling and adventure," said Otto rousing Giovanni.

The following day in the private bedchambers that Giovanni had taken upon the death of his father. With large, stained glass windows; and, three stories up, the rooms overlooked the central courtyard of the Palazzo Lascorza. They were flooded with light and commanded picturesque views of the fountains and rose bushes that comprised the beautifully maintained gardens. Off the main bedchamber lay a smaller ante chamber that now housed the Lascorza family's library. The rooms had been cleaned and aired and fresh flowers picked from the gardens below sat in long vases and their intoxicating scent filled the room. The white washed walls were adorned with paintings of long deceased notable members of the Lascorza family and at the far end of the chamber, a beautifully carved table sat close to the wall.

Hunched over the wooden desk, a dishevelled and tired Giovanni sat reading. Strewn about the ink stained desk were dozens of parchment scrolls and a thick and very ancient tome, covered in dust. The book was clad in thick dark brown leather and ornately inscribed in gold leaf and had been a prized family heirloom that had until recently sat in his father's bed chambers. Now that Giovanni had assumed the position of the head of the household, he'd had it transferred to his own. The weight of ages emanated from the pages of the book and its presence seemed to reassure the young master Lascorza. In thick gold gilt and heavy gothic style covering much of the front cover, the Latin words *Annalium genus Lascorza* told the reader that this was the *Chronicles of the Lascorza family*. Beneath that, a further sub title of *Deus Florentino constringit Noble* declared the Lascorza's to be *Noble of Florence and bound by God*. Giovanni gently toyed with the cover, running his fingers over the leather. As a boy, he recalled staring in awe at the beautifully inscribed pages replete with knightly figures committing acts of bravery and heroism as they leapt to life in his imagination.

"What are you doing?" came a familiar voice, interrupting his private thoughts.

He turned to see his new aide leaning against the door frame, busily munching on an apple.

"Hmmmm?" said Giovanni absent-mindedly.

"I said, what are you doing?" Otto wiped the mixture of spittle and mulched apple from his bushy beard.

Giovanni turned and glanced at the parchment on his table. He had, with an ink and quill, been sketching out a rough design. Although the work was far from complete, there was no doubt what it was.

Without turning to face the older man, Giovanni held the parchment in the air, as Otto walked over and took it from him.

"A gryphon?" Otto said; his low voice and accented dialect spoke with surprise. "Why have you drawn this?" he continued, handing Giovanni the parchment back.

"The Lion, was my father's insignia, the Eagle, is yours still," he replied softly. "And mine, will be the best of both. It will be gold on brightest azure."

Otto beamed. "A fine choice, though I presume you intend to keep our arms?"

Giovanni placed the feather quill down upon the table. It was done with such a delicate touch, that Otto feared what was to be said next.

"The past is beyond us, a closed chapter. The future is as yet unwritten, so it is my belief that our heraldry should change to reflect that. A man is not set in time."

In spite of his service to the coat of arms that Giovanni was so casually dismissing, Otto found himself nodding. It would be, he reassured himself, the writing of a new chapter in the history of the House Lascorza, one which he would continue to play a significant role in as the chief aide of the head of the household.

"Then, your own heraldry must take pride of place," Otto smiled.

The two men paused and an awkward silence ensued.

"What does this insignia, or these emblems mean to you, Giovanni?" said Otto again.

Giovanni gathered his thoughts. He'd grown up memorising his heraldic arms and those of the other noble families of Florence. It had been part of his upbringing and education.

"The chevron signifies the House of Lascorza," he replied, pointing at the red chevron on the azure shield.

"And what does that mean?" continued Otto.

Not entirely certain where Otto's questioning was leading, Giovanni continued.

"It is strength and protection," he replied simply.

"Is that it?"

"Is what it?" said Giovanni growing irritated, partially at Otto's repeated questioning and partially because he wasn't entirely sure what he was supposed to say.

"Is that the only thing it stands for? Is that all it means to you?" Otto continued, calmly.

Otto was rarely one to ask questions, invariably he performed whatever duties were asked of him with little care for the whys, such was his nature and such was his faith.

In this moment, however, he knew his questioning would drive his young master to further question his own decisions.

Giovanni said nothing but his furrowed brow indicated his growing annoyance.

"The chevron is permanence. It is a line, unbroken and unyielding, winding its way back to the earliest days of this family. It is strength of tradition, of name, of reputation. It is at the very core of your being. Tell me of the lion," he continued.

"It was my father's personal emblem. To signify bravery, ferocity, strength and martial valour," muttered Giovanni as he slowly began to think more laterally.

"Not just in his deeds but in his thoughts and dealings with those less fortunate than himself," Otto interjected.

Giovanni nodded.

"Most men are mere sheep, Giovanni. Desperately seeking a shepherd to guide them through the worst that life can offer. Stride amongst those men with calmness and clarity of purpose and they will instinctively follow you. This is what your father knew, this is what you must learn and become."

The young Lascorza had often regarded Otto as a loyal and pious man, short on words and quick to action, but occasionally lacking in intellect, and considered it very rare that he'd heard anything so true and poignant from him. In that moment however, he gained a level of respect for his new aide and appreciated his presence more than Otto could feasibly realise.

Giovanni pondered his words; as he was about to reply there came a loud hammering at the main entrance to the Palazzo Lascorza.

"Open the gates! Open the gates! I bring an urgent message for Giovanni Lascorza! I beg you, open the gates!"

The messenger was filthy, ragged, caked with mud having ridden hard for Florence for over a week. Panting and gasping for breath, the messenger handed over the sealed parchment.

Giovanni ripped open the seal with a sense of dread rising from the depths of his soul. His eyes scanned the contents of the parchment before he sank back down into his chair. "What? What news? Giovanni! Tell me whatever the matter is, and we shall resolve it. Surely it cannot be that grave?"

"Isabella's been kidnapped," said Giovanni numbly. "She vanished almost a week ago, not long after leaving us; she had reached Ravenna when it happened. She meant to cross the sea for the final leg of the journey to Venice, I believe."

"Pirates, then?" said Otto, worry creeping into his voice now.

"There's no mention of exactly who took her, simply that she was kidnapped and a note left by her captors," Giovanni replied as he stood up. "We have to go after her, must find her. Head to Ravenna and find out precisely what is going on," he continued absent-mindedly.

"We can't, not without permission from the Signoria. You must not forget whom we both serve now, Giovanni. I appreciate you are fond of Isabella. I may be getting on in years, but I am not blind to your feelings.

Now is not the time to rush off where angels fear to tread. Now is the time to do things by the book, and to ensure that protocol is followed."

"Protocol be damned!" shouted Giovanni.

"Giovanni listen to reason, please, I beg you," Otto implored.

"I'm listening. As my aide, I want you to go before the Signoria on my behalf, explain the circumstances, and tell them we need to leave immediately. You're more experienced at this than I am, and at this current moment in time, I'm not sure I could bear their politicking. Find a way, old friend. Make this happen. I will stay here and make the arrangements for the journey. I fear it will be a long one this time."

Realising that there would be no changing his mind, Otto made his way to the entrance to the Palazzo Lascorza, slipped out into the street and headed towards the Palazzo Vecchio.

Voices and murmuring filled the meeting chambers as the gathered members chatted idly amongst themselves, waiting for their session to commence. Otto stood nervously waiting for his chance to address them.

After a brief wait, he was called forward to address the throng. "My lords, gentlemen, I thank you for receiving me at short notice. I come before you because of a message that my master, Signor Lascorza received not thirty minutes ago, concerning our friend and former servant of Florence, Isabella Maria De Franco. She left to return to Venice almost a week ago, but alas did not reach her intended destination. It is believed that she

241

intended to make the final leg of her journey to Venice via sea, an entirely logical course of action on the face of it. It was from Ravenna that she vanished a little under a week ago, with only the briefest of notes left as a clue. My master and I seek the permission of the Signoria to go to Ravenna to uncover her whereabouts. By your leave, we can set off for Ravenna within the hour."

After some several minutes' deliberation, the Signoria decided that it was in the best interest of Florence to allow their newly appointed envoy the opportunity to proceed to Venice to strengthen trade ties, while simultaneously investigating the disappearance of their former agent.

Stepping forward, an elderly, distinguished-looking man acted as spokesman. "It is agreed, Signor Baldwinson. You have three months in which to head for Venice. You shall meet with their ruling council and remind them of their trade links with Florence on the way; it would then be prudent of you to investigate this disappearance and report back to us. In light of recent events, it would be remiss of us to not consider other enemies that may be acting against us or our best interests."

Gratefully, Otto answered, "I thank you for your forethought; we shall endeavour to increase and improve our trade relations with Venice. It shall, no doubt, serve as a useful learning experience for our new envoy."

A ripple of agreement passed through the assembly, their assent interrupted by the loud banging on a staff on the tiled floor. "You may take your leave now,

Signor Baldwinson, chief aide of Giovanni Lascorza, envoy of Florence, leave with our blessing; we wish you Godspeed and the very best of good fortune."

With their assent secured, Otto breathed a sigh of relief before hurrying from the Palazzo Vecchio.

On his return to the Palazzo Lascorza, the look of relief on Otto's face immediately lightened Giovanni's mood as he met the older man at the gate. "We have much to discuss, Giovanni. I suggest we do so somewhere where I can sit down and smoke my pipe in comfort."

In the familiar setting of Giovanni's bed chamber, Otto once again sat in the chair by the large open fire place pensively stroking his beard, whilst smoking his pipe. It was Giovanni who broke the silence. "So, we have their permission?" he inquired.

"We do. However, we're to leave for Venice at once, on the pretext that we are there to solidify our trading links. You are, after all, an envoy of this city. It will do you well to familiarise yourself with the role. Our secondary, but perhaps most important, mission will be to search for Isabella along the way. We have precisely three months in which to achieve all this."

"Three months?" retorted Giovanni. "That's hardly enough time to reach the city as it is, let alone conduct any investigation along the way!"

With a conciliatory tone in his voice, Otto nodded, "We shall simply have to make best speed for Ravenna and conduct our initial investigation there before heading for Venice. We are entitled to an armed escort; however I think we would travel faster without one. Just the two of us, so to speak. It would be unwise to upset the Signoria on our first assignment for them. Remember, De Larosa's time as Gonfaloniere of the council will end during the journey, and we will no longer enjoy his patronage."

"Then we shall just have to take our chances, trust in fate," smiled Giovanni. Otto leaned over to his left, and produced a long, slender package, wrapped in dark, navy blue velvet. "I have a gift for you, Giovanni. It is something of great value, both in terms of its sentimentality and pecuniary value."

"A gift?" replied Giovanni, the hint of surprise in his voice quite obvious. "You have no need to give me gifts. Your service to me and my family is all the gift I need."

"Ha!" retorted the old mercenary. "It is not from me. It was your father's. He wished you to have this when you were ready, when you were worthy of it."

Otto handed Giovanni the package. With his curiosity aroused, Giovanni hurriedly untied the item to reveal a longsword crafted with such ornate beauty that his mouth hung open for several moments. "It's beautiful," he breathed.

"Your father had it commissioned on his elevation to Gonfaloniere. It was his sword of state," Otto replied. "It was his wish, that you should wield it after him. You have undoubtedly proven yourself worthy of it, Giovanni."

In one fluid motion, Giovanni removed the sword from its scabbard to reveal a long and deadly sharp longsword blade made of the finest steel and carved with the intricate patterns of the Lascorza heraldic arms. The simple, elegant hilt was bedecked in silver and encrusted with rare jewels of ruby and sapphire. "I hope that I continue to prove that I am worthy of it, Otto," said Giovanni reverently.

An hour later, with letters of introduction from the Signoria safely concealed, both men were packed and saddled up, passing through the streets of Florence, heading for the northern gate. An hour after that and they were deep into the rolling Tuscan hills, on the north east road bound for Ravenna.

"I'm sure it will all be fine, Giovanni," said Otto staring at the sunset. "I have a good feeling about it. You'll see. It'll be nothing more than a false alarm. She'll have got herself lost, of that I have no doubt! Either way, a faithful companion is a sure anchor; together, we shall find the truth of the matter."

"I wish I shared your endless optimism old friend, but I cannot help this feeling in my bones that something is horribly wrong."

A grim and determined look passed over Otto's face and the two men rode on in silence.

"Besides," said Otto suddenly, "I hear Venice and Ravenna are lovely at this time of year..."

EPILOGUE

In the days that followed, the two heroes of Florence made the long and arduous journey towards Ravenna hoping to find news of their friend. The rains came early that year, as the warmth of summer passed slowly into autumn, and the world all around them became a colourful explosion of oranges and browns. Neither man knew it, but their adventures had only just begun, neither could foretell just how much their lives had changed forever. And, on the eastern horizon, mighty storm clouds gathered.

Other books by Jude Mahoney

The Ottoman Scourge - book two of "The Heroes of Florence" (US version)

The Field of Miracles - book three of "The Heroes of Florence" (US version)

UK versions

The Ottoman Scourge book two of "The Heroes of Florence" (UK version)

The Field of Miracles book three of "The Heroes of Florence" (UK version)

Printed in Great Britain
by Amazon